Heterotopia

Alternative pathways to social justice

Heterotopia

Alternative pathways to social justice

Caroline Baillie, Jens Kabo
and John Reader

Winchester, UK
Washington, USA

First published by Zero Books, 2012
Zero Books is an imprint of John Hunt Publishing Ltd., Laurel House, Station Approach,
Alresford, Hants, SO24 9JH, UK
office1@jhpbooks.net
www.johnhuntpublishing.com
www.zero-books.net

For distributor details and how to order please visit the 'Ordering' section on our website.

Text copyright: Caroline Baillie, Jens Kabo and John Reader 2012

ISBN: 978 1 78099 228 0

Design: Stuart Davies

Printed and bound by CPI Group (UK) Ltd, Croydon, CR0 4YY

We operate a distinctive and ethical publishing philosophy in all
areas of our business, from our global network of authors to
production and worldwide distribution.

CONTENTS

Chapter I

Crossing the Threshold

A Journey into New Ways of Thinking

This book is about transformations. Particularly the sort of transformations that many would like to see happen in our profession, school, community and country. Transformations that lead to shifts in ways of thinking and being, about who we are, what we do and why we do it. Many of us are disillusioned with contemporary society and how the economic drivers and dominant discourse lead us all to selfish, point-gaining behaviours. As we write this text, increasing numbers of riots, revolutions and peaceful protests are appearing on the global scene. 'Occupy Wall Street' has led to a number of other peaceful demonstrations against financial centres of major cities, which show that many members of our societies are discontented with the greed that they see in contemporary neoliberalism and are prepared to risk arrest and disruption to their lives to say so. The competitive behaviours they protest about act against community and a sense of social justice and leave us empty, bereft of direction, running in different directions at the behest of someone, but we have almost forgotten who and definitely, why. We attempt, in this short manuscript, to explore possible transformations to alternative ways of being, using a multitude of disciplinary traditions and experiences from different walks of life. We hope that it will be useful in provoking the development of a consciousness about transformation, which transcends disciplinary and professional boundaries and in starting a conversation, which will allow us to converse with each other about the changes we would like to see and how to help these happen.

What we aim to do with this text is to help find ways of

deconstructing current issues and contexts and in reconstructing alternatives, which move in more just ways. We do so, by drawing on many different disciplinary traditions as well as by using very different examples of 1) a profession, using the particular case of engineering, a practice done by highly trained workers entrusted with building services, products and systems for different parts of society, and; 2) a local community touched by, but with no power over, these professional worlds.

In our exploration of transformations to new alternatives, we began by drawing on one particular education theory, known as the 'threshold concepts framework,' which is concerned with the transition from one relatively stable state of knowing or being to another. Erik Meyer and Ray Land who originated the idea, use the terms 'liminality' or 'liminal space' to describe this transition. The term comes from the Latin 'limen' meaning passage or threshold. Liminality is a space of uncertainty and flux which different learners will navigate in different ways and with different success, some might for example get stuck, unable to move forward, while others will oscillate back and forth between different states of knowing and being. However, the kinds of transitions we are considering are not linear, not the learning of simple isolated concepts, they are messy, abstract transformations. The space, which describes the learning journey we speak of, as well as its destination, is more like a 'heterotopia.' Heterotopias are places and spaces, described by Michel Foucault in the text 'Of Other spaces' as 'non-hegemonic.' The place where Occupy Wall Street has been happening is an example of a heterotopia: a place where alternatives are considered, 'common sense' is questioned and business as usual stops for a moment. 'Hegemony,' the term coined by Gramsci, will be explored in more detail in the text but for newcomers, suffice to say that it refers to the dominant ways of thinking, propagated, reinforced and made 'common sense' by those in power in society. In this book, we invite people into this very liminal, heterotopian space so that they might rest a while and make decisions about what to do next, without being bombarded by what others seem to think are 'common sense' ways of being and thinking but which we think are madness.

In their discussion of liminality, Meyer and Land differentiate between different liminal states which is something we will expand upon in the text. One aspect of Meyer and Land's discussion is 'subliminal variation,' which they conceptualise as variation in predisposition toward knowledge building in a disciplinary knowledge area or awareness of the 'underlying game' that structures or informs a discipline. This subliminal variation will influence how learners can and will negotiate different states of liminality and thus give rise to further variation. For the purposes of this book we can interpret this subliminality in a broader sense as a person's predisposition toward engaging with the road to heterotopia. This is a way to make sense of some of our examples of certain books we picked up or people we met who resonated with our selves greatly, despite the sometime randomness of the first encounter. After all most of us (most people) have picked up books or met new people by chance, but (potentially) it is our states of subliminality that influences how we engage them. Jack Mezirow, a founding figure regarding transformative learning theory, most likely would connect this to different habits of mind that influence our frames of reference and points of view. One key point of this book then is that when we become aware of (aspects of) our own subliminal predispositions we increase our possibilities to act and further transform our subliminality and selves. This is reflected in how we (in addition to chance meetings with texts and people) also consciously seek out certain new texts or people who might help us grow or continue to develop as individuals and part of communities.

In 1964 Marshall McLuhan told us that 'the media is the message.' In other words, he was claiming that the manner of doing things is itself integral to the content being expressed. In this book, the subject matter will be presented in a manner consistent with the ideas being described. This may sound simple, but it creates challenges for both authors and readers. This introduction will lay out the contours of the discussion and the range of material to be encountered. We will do so in part by each author speaking from their own positions and experiences (John, Caroline, Jens) where these are different from each other.

We are going to explore transformations, what is possible, what we think about it, what terms we might need, what thresholds we have to cross, when acting as a socially just citizen or 'professional' in our current societies. In the text we will be using 'engineering' as an example of a profession whose work affects everything that we do, how we act and behave on a day to day basis. The way we approach our critique of engineering may be applied to any such profession (law, medicine, commerce etc.) so we hope to make it as accessible as possible to any reader. This transformation is mediated by the dialogues between an engineering academic who initiated the 'Engineering, Social Justice, and Peace' network (ESJP) (Caroline) and an engineering education scholar (Jens) in order to question the dominant paradigms in their profession. These transformations and our way of thinking about them is then critiqued and informed by our third author, a public theologian with expertise in political economics and sociology (John) and who deals on a daily basis with the aftermath of global and local 'professional' economic, educational, medical, farming and other intangible decisions and policies. John is at the receiving end of the practices of the politicians, professionals and policy makers. We see these as very different angles or lenses onto the same problem.

Throughout the text, we reflect from a theoretical perspective on the issues and questions raised, we apply these to engineering as an example of the profession under study and we additionally ground this by transferring the ideas to personal experiential and down to earth contexts (indicated by text in quotation marks and in **different font**). We hope, in this way, to assist readers, as they move into the liminal space, to learn through experience of variation. Lets look at this idea of variation in relation to a child learning about colour. Variation theory suggests that we understand 'red' by the existence of 'blue' and by varying around the critically important aspects we get to understand these. Showing the child a variety of red objects so they can see that red remains the same, whilst the object itself changes (red book, red shoe etc.), then showing them a red book, a blue book, a yellow book etc. will help them see the difference between 'red' and 'book.' Hence we will present very different lenses to view the same phenomena, in order to describe the variation to be experienced, thereby highlighting its critical features.

As a result, what follows draws upon ideas and theories from a wide range of sources, some of which may be less familiar than others, some of which are very academic, others very practical and down to earth. We are aware that this presents a unique challenge to those who are more comfortable within their own particular discipline, or indeed are not engaged in academic discourse and its peculiar conventions, as well as those who are! We intend to make it clear where material comes from so that readers can pursue this for themselves if they wish. Since it is central to our argument however, that development and transformation are more likely to occur when different ideas are brought into contact and new combinations of thoughts and insights emerge, we do not intend to produce a grand theory about how these different ideas should be harmonised or brought together. On the contrary, it is consistent with our argument that concepts and notions that may not obviously or neatly fit together be brought into contact in order that what we call our 'heterotopian liminal space' might be understood. Even as authors, we are also in this space, experiencing it differently from one another.

5

"My first appreciation of 'liminal space' was termed, 'hanging out in the fog' after picking up a book by Guy Claxton entitled *The Wayward Mind: An Intimate History of the Unconscious*. Although this particular phrase does not appear in the book itself, he uses it on websites and educational programmes to describe the learning process that he advocates. As it happens it resonated at the time with a local community project that I called 'The Big Idea' (not to be confused with 'The Big Society'), which included at one point taking a coach load of people up onto the edge of the Peak District (in the UK) overlooking the village we had come from in order to place the settlement in the context of the wider geography of the area. As it happened, that particular day the Peak District fog descended with a vengeance and the participants were completely unable to see the next blade of grass let alone the village below! Yet, as with so many of these projects, a good time was had by all, and the British spirit triumphed over climatic adversity. What we ended up doing was, quite literally, hanging out in the fog, so the image was a powerful one." (John)

Guy Claxton suggests that in order to learn, grow and develop, it is necessary to enter a 'zone of entanglement' or what we are calling a 'liminal space'(assuming one is not there already) and not worry about trying to find our way out quickly or prematurely. In the book, *The Wayward Mind* he backs this with up with detailed references to the history of our understanding of the human mind, making it clear that similar ideas about human creativity have been circulating for generations despite the cultural and intellectual differences. Amongst other writers, he refers to John Keats and his notion of 'negative capability': 'that is, when man is capable of being in uncertainties, mysteries, doubts, without any irritable reaching after fact and reason.' So one can let go of the need to be in control of the processes of one's own mind, can welcome confusion and the spontaneous swirling of ideas, sink down towards the unconscious and experience the benefits of doing so. Claxton links this to the ideas of other Romantics such as Blake and Hazlitt, and also to elements of the Christian mystical tradition: the 'apophatic way' or the 'via negativa.' One enters 'the cloud of unknowing' and thereby moves closer to that which is beyond definition or description.

'Heterotopia' is thus our starting point and our goal for this book. We will be discussing ways in which we understand trans-formations into, through and beyond such spaces, which allow us the freedom to be 'counter hegemonic' or question the dominant common sense of this millennia. We will be exploring a heterotopia in which engineers might find themselves if they wished to be more responsive, socially just professionals. We will look at this heterotopia through different lenses and these will in turn be the topic of each chapter. A brief introduction to each of these lenses is described below.

The first lens will be a critical lens, to be encountered in chapter 2, following a tradition of critical theories (the many different traditions of critique emanating originally from the Frankfurt school of Critical Theory) that of how to critique and move beyond the accepted or conventional wisdom within a specific field. For all the authors, Paulo Freire has been extremely important. Freire makes a distinction between the 'banking concept' of education, where the teacher or expert attempts to 'deposit' ideas or truth in the mind of pupils, and the notion of 'dialogical education,' where all students are treated as adults and what they bring to the process is seen as crucial. This was formative for all authors. What Freire offers is a process which is not in the control of the existing power structures but which potentially releases the more subversive ideas and experiences of those who are 'on the receiving end' of that power, hence it has the possibility of being not only dialogical but also profoundly democratic. His worked examples from Latin America are of great interest, but they do raise the issue of how this might operate in very different cultural and political context, which was, and still is, very real for those of us who wanted to use ideas from Freire or Liberation Theology in an affluent setting.

In chapter 3, we refer to the work of Antonio Gramsci and his concept of hegemony, and therefore implicitly the means by which the power of ideas to impose interpretations, and therefore practices, on others, can be challenged. We find Gramsci's notion of the 'organic intellectual' of equal use. This is the idea that those who resist need to be directly involved in grass roots action and not simply detached intellectuals coming up with grand theories that bear little relationship to the realities on the front line. All three authors of this book aim to fit the bill of 'Counter hegemonic organic intellectuals'!

Following from our interest in Gramsci's work and also the scholar Ludwik Fleck, who introduced the ideas of 'thought collectives' and 'thought styles,' we question the 'common sense' that is to be encountered in the discipline of engineering. This is the 'common sense' which is socially constructed by the dominant ideas of the time. In everyday jargon we use the term to mean 'sensible,' following our knowledge and judgement. This sounds good but of course if our judgement is 'constructed' by others or by our social context and upbringing, we need to question the motives and values of the society in which we find ourselves, before deciding if indeed following our 'common sense' is the most appropriate thought or action. Hence the idea of common sense in this way takes on a more sinister meaning. The implication of this for our story is that certain ideas or ways of looking at the world, in this case the link between engineering and capitalism, become the accepted or conventional wisdom within the profession, so much so that people are not even aware that there might be alternative perspectives. It is just taken for granted that the main purpose of engineering, in this case, is to serve the interests of business and the profit motive. Other views do still exist, but they tend to get filtered out because 'common sense' prevails.

We are keen to show that similar ideas occur in other disciplines and that there is value in making these links and drawing upon wider resources in what the philosopher Wittgenstein might consider to be 'family resemblances.' So one is not arguing that these are all the same, but only that there are enough similarities to make the comparisons fruitful and interesting.

There are parallels here with the concept of plausibility structures as described in Peter Berger's book *A Rumour of Angels*. A plausibility structure is a framework of interpretation or understanding which has become the accepted wisdom within a field of study and makes it possible for some things to be believed and others to be dismissed as not believable. An example of this would be the idea of the miracle. If one holds to a strict view of the laws of nature which says that they cannot be broken, then clearly miracles simply cannot happen and any evidence that they do has to be either dismissed or redefined. Another example is the positivist mindset in science. If scientists are looking for one objective truth that fits within 'known' scientific models, they will reject new data which does not fit as 'outliers.' The effect of this is to create a dogmatic approach to the world, which rules certain possibilities out in advance.

A similar idea occurs within the philosophy of science and the debates initiated by Thomas Kuhn back in the 1960s when he introduced the notion of paradigms into science, in his book *The Structure of Scientific Revolutions*. He was also arguing that one can identify certain frameworks of interpretation or ways of understanding how the world is, that become the accepted wisdom, and that one can describe this as new paradigms becoming dominant in scientific study. This then led to heated debates about how precisely this happens. Can it be described as a rational process of some sort where there is suddenly enough evidence to shift the belief system and the 'old order' is no longer credible or acceptable, or is the process much more random and contingent upon extra-scientific factors? This latter view was presented by Feyerabend in a book called *Against Method*, which presented historical evidence to suggest that science 'progresses' in a much more haphazard and unpredictable way, and that narratives telling it otherwise are constructed after the event in order to justify the position being promoted.

What this makes clear is that the subject of power is central to the discussions in this book, even though it is not addressed directly by the authors. Breaking out of the thought styles, paradigms or plausibility structures and initiating innovative thought and practice is as much about how to resist existing power structures as it is about actual content, one could argue. As such, we refer to the work of Foucault and his notion of regimes of truth, as well as his considerable work on power itself. Particularly illuminating is his suggestion that power is not simply a zero-sum game, so that if one person or group has power then it is always at the expense of another person or group, but that power is more like the air we breathe. Power acts like a series of flows or forces in relation to which humans are located differently but always have the possibility of accessing. Thus nobody is ever 'powerless' even if they choose not to tap into the power that is available to them. There is always power and counter-power and thus the possibility of resistance. If this has some validity then it offers a more optimistic prospect for challenge and change, and that is something that all the authors of this book advocate and want to work towards.

Another philosopher whom we have found helpful in this context is Jacques Derrida. In particular, the idea of 'deconstruction' can be seen as another means by which existing and established interpretations can be opened up and challenged. This is the very approach that Caroline has introduced into engineering classes to enable students to think counter hegemonically. The word deconstruction itself needs to be treated with caution though and is often employed too easily and loosely by those who claim to be followers of Derrida but have not entered into his work rigorously enough. Derrida himself makes it clear that there is no one thing called deconstruction which one can then define and employ as some sort of emancipatory technique. One does not 'deconstruct' some concept or use of language and thereby automatically create its liberating opposite. It is more like showing in individual instances that alternative interpretations always exist beneath the surface of the conventional wisdom and are part of the original term in question. But there is never a simple reversal of meaning that overturns the existing one.

As with Foucault, this does suggest that the way to challenge power does not consist of overturning or reversing it, because one then simply replaces one set of power relationships with another. There are significant political and educational implications of this view. Rather than a straightforward overthrow of what exists, change is more likely to occur through a process of opening up which does not determine in advance what an outcome should or might be. We enter into a heterotopia. Hence one returns to the question of human agency and control. One does not destroy A by replacing it with B. One opens up the alternative possibilities already existing in A through a process of radical thought and engagement with other ideas, but without knowing where this will lead. Change is not a linear process, but essentially nonlinear and unpredictable.

The other parallel in this chapter comes from the discipline of hermeneutics, or interpretation theory, as to be encountered in recent European philosophy and the work of Heidegger, Gadamer and Habermas.

Put simply there are two major conclusions that can be reached from this. First, interpretation operates in something like a circle; one has to start somewhere with some accepted views in order to even begin the process of interpretation. There are assumptions from which one then works outwards and that have not themselves been justified by the process itself. It is possible that these might in due course be called into question, but then the process has to begin all over again starting from different assumptions. Second, interpretation happens within a 'community of interpreters,' certainly in all academic disciplines. In this way individual or idiosyncratic interpretations can and will be checked against what the majority of one's colleagues accept as being true at that particular time.

This again raises the question of how much freedom or flexibility exists within a particular field or discipline when it comes to 'thinking new thoughts' or being creative or transformative. How does change actually come about and what costs are involved for those who would initiate it? To 'swim against the tide' in any thought field is a risky and costly business and one appreciates that some innovative thinkers have not been recognised or their views accepted in their own lifetimes. It also poses the deeper philosophical question of 'what is truth or is there indeed one truth'?

The initial common ground between the three authors came out of discussions about the educational process in their respective fields and the prospects for change and transformation, summed up in their use of the terms 'threshold concept' (troublesome and transformatory concept) and 'liminal space.' There is a shared assumption and common experience that change can and does happen, and that people can, under certain circumstances, begin to see and think differently. Much of the task then is to try to identify the conditions and circumstances, which enable this to happen, and these will be described in greater detail in the rest of the book.

In chapter 4 we consider the various models, theories, ideas, and metaphors that we and other writers use to think about change and transformation. We reflect upon models for the nonlinearity of learning as well as the model of a poppy seed head scattering seeds to the wind as a metaphor for personal and community development. We then move into the reflections of others. To help us in our quest for transformation through the 'liminal space' and into broader debates on radical change we access and contrast the work of Alain Badiou and Gilles Deleuze. For the sake of completeness, we also draw brief attention to the more recent work of the philosopher Slavoj Zizek, who has taken over the mantle of Derrida of late through a series of regular publications and media appearances. Although even more difficult to pin down in many ways, some of Zizek's ideas have resonances with those just mentioned. His work tends to be less optimistic, if anything, and offers less hope of genuinely emancipatory action, but is perhaps a necessary counterpoint to the ideas, which emerged during the 1970s and 1980s. Using concepts from the French psychoanalyst Lacan, but also influenced by Hegel and Marx, Zizek suggests that replacing one set of dominant influences by another is not going to contribute to human progress. He even questions whether replacing one 'Master Signifier,' which is the term he uses to describe the dominant forces in the human psyche, by another, is possible, or whether it is better to leave that location in the human mind empty. Whilst not making matters clearer, Zizek does perhaps offer a necessary note of caution about what can actually be achieved by the struggles for freedom and change that fellow social activists and philosophers have advocated. Once again, there is a question of human autonomy and control and of how much can realistically be expected of political activity and radical thought.

This is where the process becomes more random and more challenging. All the authors would argue that the material mentioned so far has contributed to their own process of drawing on other people's ideas to try to open up the processes of thought and activity, both for themselves and for those they have been working with. So we have presented different layers of words and ideas gleaned from a range of sources, that, at one time or another, have helped in thinking new thoughts.

It has been said, more often by perceptive four year olds commenting on how adults use language, that we should create new words so that new things can happen. This is the spirit in which we offer this book. Language is itself dynamic and changes organically, but is also subject to deliberate development as those on the edge struggle to express their experiences. Shakespeare has been credited with creating 3000 new English words, for instance, sometimes through neologisms, bringing together existing terms in new and unexpected combinations. It has also been suggested that, by doing this, he widened the range of emotions that humans (or at least English speakers) were then able to identify and express.

It is clearly true that language continues to develop and, by doing so, enables us to articulate and experience ourselves and the world differently. One of our shared concerns is that the 'conventional wisdom' within certain disciplines acts as a strait-jacket and a cover for power structures, thus inhibiting and restricting the changes and challenges that ought to be possible. So we will set about creating and using new counter hegemonic terms which have been created, in order to enable the flexibility of thought and practice that could change our world for the better. We will attempt to enter heterotopia. To aid the reader with the language we use, we have created a glossary of terms which we might call 'threshold concepts,' which can be troublesome to understand but potentially transformatory; they will open up new and different ways of thinking. This will include some terms very familiar to some and not to others. However, as we wish to help the reader enter 'liminal space' and not to pass through we are not offering 'definitions' of these terms. They are simply highlighted, to say, 'we know these are new and strange terms, they have multiple meanings which you can start to explore, and by accepting that you will take a while to fully comprehend how you understand them, you will be entering your own heterotopia.' The glossary can be found at the end of the book.

One of the most valuable aspects of the work of Deleuze by himself, and it needs to be noted that this is different in important respects from the work he did with Felix Guattari, is his capacity to invent new words and new ideas that unsettle and confuse. At a later stage we will point out how terms such as 'state science' versus 'nomad science,' 'smooth spaces' versus 'striated spaces' and 'holey spaces,' and many others, potentially suggest common ground and open up new ways of thinking about the world. It is like having to learn a new language in order to try to work out what he is getting at. But then, the same is true of struggling with Foucault and Derrida. Is it worth the effort, or is this just clever people messing about with words?

Heather Menizies would give a resounding 'yes' to the first question, and we refer now to her book *Whose brave new world?*, where she demonstrates clearly how language can confine and prescribe. Referring to George Orwell's *1984*, she worries that, just like using a term such as 'double double plus' to replace an adjective such as 'beautiful' and 'tantalising,' in order to control the emotions of the 'Proles,' we currently use language such as 'capitalising' and 'profiting' in place of 'benefiting' so that eventually we think they are one and the same. This is how our common sense gets generated.

Disciplinary domains are often the boundaries for the sort of common sense or thought styles, which define the language and tacit knowing of the tribe. The authors described above, especially Deleuze, offer a different perspective and explicitly break boundaries of all kinds, whilst writing about the boundaries themselves. It is clear then that in order to work in an emancipatory way, in order to break as many boundaries to knowing as possible, to break free from a thought style and to really consider multiple ways of being and knowing, ultimately we need to try to think through other ontologies or *ways of being*. We will not attempt to do this within this book, but acknowledge that we are privileging a Western knowledge system and worldview and know that we are necessarily limited in this.

In creating new words, we are creating new ways of thinking, opening up new patterns and consciousness. We would argue that new thoughts and language offer us one way in which one can move out beyond the 'enclosures' created by the thought styles and towards and through the 'thresholds' into other ideas and actions presented by more radical thinkers. Those of us who try to enter other disciplinary domains, know that the reception is often hostile, with a resounding 'you don't understand that thinker in the right way.' We need to carefully balance on the knife edge of creating our own boundaries whilst trying to break down others.

After hanging out in the fog for four chapters, we imagine that our reader will at this point be well and truly in a heterotopia. We invite you, in chapter 5, to consider a reconceptualisation, a new common sense, for engineering as a profession, which we hope may reflect somewhat on other disciplines also.

Throughout the text, we attempt to make explicit the principles on which we believe that engineering as a profession could operate, if it were to become a just profession, as well as reflecting on the difficulties of getting to that place. We all three reflect upon the work of others in disparate disciplines and how that feeds into our practical endeavours. There are a number of objectives at stake here: 1) to show that the concepts we are using have direct and practical implications and are not simply attractive ideas without any useful application 2) to link the search for social justice and concern to give a voice to those who are marginalised, from within engineering to wider spheres of activity in order to encourage others to engage in this type of heterotopian action 3) to reinforce the notion of the counter hegemonic organic intellectual by arguing that theory and practice come together through human responses to situations of injustice and exploitation 4) to suggest that at the heart of these debates and projects lie a number of assumptions that need to be made more explicit. These include our understanding of the way the world is; notions of how change can come about; the nature and role of power; and 5) our understanding of what it is to be or become a just and conscious human being.

It is the last of these which emerges as a constant theme through our writing and action. When we talk about liminal spaces, threshold concepts and 'hanging out in the fog,' what we are saying is that there are limits to the extent to which humans are in conscious and deliberate control of what happens. It is when humans attempt to determine, control and manipulate the lives of others that injustice and exploitation are most likely to emerge, and, by contrast, when they are most willing to experiment, spend time out in the fog and to let go of their predetermined ideas that creativity, growth and transformation are most likely to result. Both the ideas on which we draw and the practices in which we are engaged bring this lesson home again and again. This is why we wish to share our experience of heterotopia.

Chapter 2

Critique of Established Positions

What is this profession called 'engineering'?

We have decided in this book to use the profession of engineering, which we believe is in need of critical and urgent transformation, to test out our ideas. But if we are to use a profession such as engineering to view our concerns, we will need to start by exploring what engineering might be conceived to be in today's society.

Engineering is both a *profession*, to be an engineer, and an *activity*, to engineer. A classical definition of engineering was devised by Thomas Tredgold on behalf of the Institution of Civil Engineers in 1828 that equates engineering with 'the art of directing the great sources of power in nature for the use and convenience of man.' A more recent definition of engineering is given by the American Engineering Accreditation Commission (ABET):

Engineering is the profession in which a knowledge of the mathematical and natural sciences, gained by study, experience, and practice, is applied with judgement to develop ways to utilize, economically, the materials and forces of nature for the benefit of mankind.

The last part of the ABET definition rings very similar to Tredgold's 180 years older version. The purpose of engineers is still to control the forces of nature for the convenience of humans, but now with the added emphasis for this to be done economically. Another aspect has also entered the definition, the idea of engineers applying knowledge of mathematics and science to achieve their goals. In Canada the corresponding agency to the ABET is the Canadian Engineering Accreditation Board, which offers the following view of engineering and engineering education:

> The engineering profession expects of its members' competence in engineering, as well as an understanding of the effect of engineering on society. Thus, accredited engineering programs must contain not only adequate mathematics, science and engineering, but they must also develop communication skills and an understanding of the environmental, cultural, economic and social impacts of engineering on society and of the concept of sustainable development.

The emphasis here is on the notion that engineers must understand the impacts of their practice on society and the environment, which stands in strong contrast to Tredgold's definition, which can be interpreted in a way that nature exists for humans to exploit. The European Enlightenment era left an imprint on all disciplinary fields, and the field of engineering was notably influenced. Many engineers see their work in positivist terms, even if they do not actually work in this way. Like many scientists, they take it for granted that their work is objective, and they see a huge division between the logic of their machines and the subjectivity of human beings. Some scholars have argued that as a result engineers have been employed as hired guns, at the behest of political rulers and wealthy corporations. Johnston and associates in their book *Engineering and Society* deem that the definition of engineering, should be 'A total societal enterprise, with significant influences on all aspects of human life and a major role to play in moving the world towards particular goals.' The problem comes when the 'particular goals' of the political rulers and wealthy corporations do not match the needs of the majority of the people who should be served by engineering.

If we would like engineering to serve people and the needs of all people, we must then ask the question: 'what would engineering look like if it were to focus first and foremost on people and not profit?' We can 'critique' engineering through a 'critical lens' of 'social justice.'

Mapping out the critical lens

We are using the term 'critique' in reference to the application of critical theory. The critical theorists of the Frankfurt School, such as Theodor W. Adorno, Max Horkheimer and Herbert Marcuse, are the originators of 'Critical Theory' and influenced the resulting critical social theories, which use a multitude of radical and less radical lenses through which to analyse social situations.

Rather perversely, however, when the term 'critical thinking' or 'ability to think critically' is used in the context of engineering, it is often assumed to refer to thinking clearly and rationally, and usually within the dominant discourse. This can actually result in the opposite of what we intend here, as what is seen as 'rational,' is often bounded within what is common sense within a given thought style. Emerging from critical theory, then, the term critical thinking takes on a different and more urgent meaning: the ability to see beyond what we consider to be 'common sense.'

So developing a critical consciousness and critical thinking to enable 'praxis' (moving beyond critique to action) suggests the use of a 'critical lens' for looking at the world. In our own work we use the idea of social justice as a critical lens for engineers to look at their practice and profession and to begin to enter the heterotopia of alternatives.

In an extensive review in her book *Engineering and Social Justice*, Donna Riley explores a range of perspectives and movements that fall under the umbrella of social justice, ranging from faith traditions and human rights to ecology and critical theories, such as feminism and critical race theory. She acknowledges that it is difficult to define the term social justice. She tells us that 'it is not that the term is poorly understood... each of us knows what we mean by it. The problem is that the term resists a concise and permanent definition. Its mutability and multiplicity are... key characteristics of social justice.'

Sharon Gewirtz in 'Mapping the Territory' argues that (social) justice has two dimensions, one distributional and one relational. According to her, discussions of social justice often become synonymous with discussions of how material and monetary resources are distributed in society. A more holistic approach to social justice also reflects the nature of the relationships which structure society. As an example of a holistic synthesis of the two dimensions Gewirtz puts forward Iris Marion Young's idea of the 'five faces of oppression': *exploitation* (benefiting at the expense of others), *marginalisation* (being pushed away from participation in social life), *powerlessness* (being unable to make one's voice heard due to lack of status or respect), *cultural imperialism* (the dominant culture becomes the way of interpreting social life) and *violence* (the risk and reality of being targeted with acts of violence). Both Gewirtz and Young agree that these are all mechanisms of oppression and social injustice and that these need to be addressed and countered when working to promote social justice. We adopt these considerations of social justice to frame our 'critical lens.'

Critical theories of transformation within engineering education

The main work of Caroline and Jens is to critique the engineering profession through a critical lens of social justice and thereby develop a critical pedagogy for engineering education. If there is to be a critical repositioning of a profession such as engineering, this needs to start with a new generation of engineering students. We need to ask ourselves, as educators, how can we break free from the hegemony engineering currently experiences? How, instead, could engineering be focused around social justice? And how do we help our students see through a lens of social justice to critique their chosen profession?

Progressive educator bell hooks tells us in her book *Teaching to Transgress* that 'critical thinking (is) the primary element allowing for the possibility of change (within ourselves and society)... without the capacity to think critically about ourselves and our lives, none of us would be able to move forward, to change, to grow.' As an example hooks reflects on progressive education in *Teaching Community*:

Progressive professors did not need to indoctrinate students and teach them that they should oppose domination. Students came to these positions via their own capacity to think critically and assess the world they live in. Progressive educators discussing issues of imperialism, race, gender, class, and sexuality heightened everyone's awareness of the importance of these concepts (even those individuals who did not share our perspective). That awareness has created the conditions for concrete change, even if those conditions are not yet known to everyone.

hooks argues in the same book that her experience as an educator has shown her 'how easy it is for individuals to change their thoughts and actions when they become aware and when they desire to use that awareness to alter behaviour.' Her key point is that 'where there is consciousness there is choice.'

Freire has been a key influence for most critical pedagogues who aim to transform society to be more socially just, through 'critical' pedagogy. Freire's work stems from the perceived need to develop a theoretical framework to support educational practice for a less oppressive society. In his seminal work *Pedagogy of the Oppressed* Freire put forward the core of his framework: what he calls conscientizacao, which refers to learning to perceive social, political and economic contradictions, and to take action against the oppressive elements of reality. In English the term becomes conscientisation, or the process of developing a critical consciousness.

Freire differentiates between what he calls banking and problem posing or dialogical education. In banking education the relationship between teacher and students is hierarchical and knowledge is a gift from those who consider themselves knowledgeable to those they consider to know nothing. Banking education is not a way to help students develop a critical consciousness, but rather serves to preserve the status quo. Problem posing education, on the other hand, aims to break the hierarchical relationship between students and teacher and is a vehicle for developing a critical consciousness. The growth process takes the form of respectful and non-oppressive dialogue, which aims to help people develop their power to perceive critically the way they exist in the world with which and in which they find themselves. Key to Freire's work was the role of the oppressed in society. Central to his reasoning is that any true change toward a less oppressive society has to start with the oppressed. Freire was (initially) working with a class perspective, which is clearly still very important today, however his work has been used to consider various forms of oppression and the approaches that education can take to empower.

"My first encounter with Freire's work was accidental in that I was browsing a bookshop in Manchester and came across his *Pedagogy of the Oppressed*. It looked interesting and radical so I bought it. (Jens notes that this is the subliminal predisposition at work as discussed previously). Parts of it immediately began to make sense while other bits were less accessible. My concern at the time was the distance between institutions and those who operate within them, and the people for whom those institutions claimed to operate and for whose benefit they were supposed to function. It seemed to me that, at grass roots level, people were turned into passive recipients of the services that the professionals either chose or were conditioned into offering and that no recognition was given to the actual needs on the ground.

What Freire seemed to be offering was an understanding of both power and communication that provided an alternative model whereby ordinary people could gain the confidence to articulate their own needs and indeed feelings about what was happening. So it was not simply a matter of thinking through the implications of the different models of adult education, the banking versus the dialogical concept, but also of enabling people who were traditionally on the receiving end of various welfare services to gain a voice in the process. I will give an example of this.

I visited an old lady whose son had died recently. This happened just before Christmas and the weather was very cold and frosty. It was the son who had dealt with all the practical heating needs in his mother's council (local regional government authority) bungalow on one of their large estates, and who had also contacted the council when necessary. When I saw her, she had an electric fire in one room and the rest of the property was cold because the heating system had broken down. It was obvious that she was at risk of hypothermia and she had no idea how to contact the council to get anything done. At that stage I also had no experience of dealing with council staff or who to contact, so I went home, did some homework and made some phone calls. Having got the usual 'holding' answer and promise that the problem would be addressed, I then left the matter for a few days. When I visited again, however, a few days later, nothing had happened and nobody had been to call. At this point I made contact with somebody with greater experience who said that the only way to deal with this was to threaten to phone the local press and to make sure that the story was on the front pages. One phone call to the council along those lines did indeed elicit the appropriate action and the problem was dealt with.

I began to wonder what sort of system this was that required that sort of threat before action was taken. How should the care of those in need be properly catered for and in what ways did the bureaucratic mechanisms and mindsets in place actually inhibit that process? What apparently had to happen was somebody coming into that situation as a catalyst or troublemaker and speaking on behalf of the particular person in need. But then what about all those other individuals who did not have anybody to speak on their behalf? There needed to be some way in which the established systems could be disrupted and disturbed and which would allow people themselves to articulate their problems and requirements. It looked to me as though Freire's ideas, based on his own practice with marginalised groups in South America, had something important to say about this. Although I would not have used the language then, it was moving towards creating those liminal spaces or points of uncertainty and transition where new and creative activity could take place. At this stage I did not know that Freire had been an influence upon the development of Liberation Theology, but, in due course, I began to see how this was the case." (John)

Transformations and thresholds

While awareness might be a necessary condition for change, we need to remember that, for Freire, conscientizacao had two dimensions: 'to come to see' and 'to take action.' Wilfred Carr and Stephen Kemmis in their book *Becoming Critical* point out that a process of critique can transform consciousness (ways of viewing the world) without necessarily changing practice in the world. In order to help us with the transformation process, we draw on two other educational theories: transformative learning and threshold concepts. Asking engineering students to look through a critical lens has the potential to be a troublesome and/or transformative experience since their ideas of themselves and their future profession are likely to be challenged, in other words it will not be easy for most of them. Jack Mezirow, who coined the phrase 'transformative learning,' describes in his chapter 'Learning to think like an adult' in the book *Learning as Transformation*, three related meaning structures: frames of reference, habits of mind and points of view. He defines these in the following ways: 1) 'A frame of reference is a 'meaning perspective,' the structure of assumptions and expectations through which we filter sense impressions... (It) is composed of two dimensions, a habit of mind and resulting points of view.' 2) 'A habit of mind is a set of assumptions—broad, generalized, orienting predispositions that act as a filter for interpreting the meaning of experience... (It) becomes expressed as a point of view.' 3) 'A point of view comprise clusters of meaning schemas— sets of immediate specific expectations, beliefs, feelings, attitudes, and judgements—that tacitly direct and shape a specific interpretation and determine how we judge, typify objects, and attribute causality.'

Who we are is closely associated with the frames of reference we hold and changing or transforming these are often nontrivial. For Mezirow, critical reflection is the key to any significant shifts of frames of reference. However, he points out that subjective reframing commonly involves an intensive and difficult emotional struggle as old perspectives become challenged and transformed. Therefore it is important for educators to recognise the importance of a supportive environment to facilitate critical reflection and acting on any insights gained.

The troublesome nature of the transformation is explicitly dealt with in the threshold concepts framework. This is a growing body of educational knowledge which focuses on learning as passing through thresholds and enabling students to consider new and different ways of seeing the world. The assumption made within the threshold concepts framework initiated by educational researchers Erik Meyer and Ray Land, is that there are in most or all (disciplinary) knowledge domains certain concepts that serve as gateways to further progress as a learner and a deeper level of knowledge. The idea is that part of the process of grasping a threshold concept is that learners change the way they see the subject or part thereof and potentially themselves (in relation to the subject). The changes in thinking and seeing are what open up previously inaccessible knowledge areas. Meyer and Land suggest that the process to grasp a threshold concept also brings learners to adopt the ways of thinking and practising of the disciplinary community of practice in question.

The term 'concept' does not necessarily have to be interpreted in the narrow sense. For example, social justice is not a concept in the same sense as gravity or complex numbers are concepts in engineering; rather it represents a way of seeing the world. Not in itself a critical pedagogy, the most useful aspect of the threshold concepts framework for our purposes has been the term liminality, which is a space of uncertainty, flux and transition between two more stable states of knowing, being or seeing. By acknowledging that learners will navigate a particular liminal space in different ways and with different success, some might, for example, get stuck unable to move forward, Meyer, Land and Peter Davies introduced the notion of variation and different states of liminality. They discuss preliminal, liminal, postliminal and subliminal variation, that is variation in the ways in which students see the concept come into focus, pass through the threshold, come out the other side, and their predisposition for knowledge building in the discipline. In our work we have re-framed this somewhat by introducing the notion of a continuous liminal spectrum, which goes from preliminal to postliminal. An illustration of this can be seen in Figure 1.

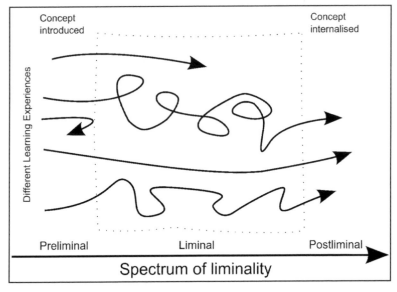

Figure 1: A visual representation of the variation present among students navigating a liminal space connected to a threshold. Some might pass through without much effort, while others take more winding paths that might also involve much backtracking. Yet others might get stuck or choose not to engage with the concept any further upon first encountering it.

An important aspect of our work to note is that whilst in conventional interpretations of threshold concepts, the focus is often on acquiring established ways of thinking and practicing, our aim is to introduce new ways of thinking and seeing into engineering. Based on our research we suggest that current dominant engineering 'common sense' can serve as a barrier toward social justice and thus social justice can be seen as a threshold which when traversed could potentially change the profession. Our goal as educators is to understand the barriers to the development of a socially just lens and pathways around these into heterotopia.

A worked example from engineering education

One particular course which Caroline introduced into two different Universities, Queen's University in Canada and the University of Western Australia, 'Engineering and Social Justice,' was specifically intended to help students pass through the threshold and see engineering through a lens of social justice. Engineering and social science students took the course together. In line with Freire's conscientizacao the aim of the course was not only to raise awareness among the students of social justice, but also to help them engage with the issues raised and shift their ways of looking at themselves, their profession, and the world. Students were interviewed about their thinking related to engineering, early and late in the term. In addition, student self-reflections on the course were collected. Among the engineering students in the class, seven different but related, articulations of changing perspectives on engineering could be discerned. These were:

A: Critique of the hegemony of engineering education
B: Critique of the hegemony of the current profit paradigm of engineering
C: Critique of the notion of a 'right answer'
D: Critique of the 'common sense' of technical solutions
E: The need for engineers to be humble and open to critique
F: The need to ask who do we, as engineers, engineer for?
G: The world is confusing and how do we as engineers fit in?

The theme running through all of these were the deconstruction of the students' original perceptions of engineering. Below we give some examples of student quotes for each theme.

A: Critique of the hegemony of engineering education

In the engineering curriculum we are programmed to

determine an answer and we are not always asked to question the situation at hand. In general the questions of why this task is being performed and who it is affecting are simply not asked. I feel as if this class has helped me to be more critical of different situations I face, and I found that this class was very informative and eye-opening.

Here the critical aspect is the focus on how current engineering education promotes a certain limited way of thinking, which, for example, favours problem solving over problem posing.

B: Critique of the hegemony of the current profit paradigm of engineering

It's the social, environmental and economic… some companies have tried to go for it, but I think that it might be one of the most important things for an engineer to consider the true bottom line and (that) it's not just about the money. And to think about what are the social implications and the environmental implications and how there are gains and losses from all of them.

Here the critical aspect is the focus on how current engineering practice usually is strongly aligned with a purely economical perspective on the expense of social and environmental considerations.

C: Critique of the notion of a 'right answer'

(The course) taught me that my opinions and my ideas don't necessarily have to be right or wrong as they very often are measured and considered in engineering, right answer, wrong answer, and it's just very weird to think 'oh! here's an idea and that's all it is,' it's just an idea, it's not an answer or right or wrong... you could judge it accordingly.

Here the critical aspect is the focus on how there exists in engineering education a notion that there always is a 'right' in any given situation rather than that there can be several 'right' answers depending on one's perspective and context.

D: Critique of the 'common sense' of technical solutions

Knowing the underlying social cause of the problem changes the way in which the problem can be dealt with. Critical examination of social causes rather than a focus on only technical problems is something I never considered before, although now that I think about it, it appears to be in fact much more important than the technological factors alone... (The project) has changed my perspective on social issues and has led me to believe that the engineering approach to problem solving taught at (University) is generally not the most comprehensive and is severely lacking in social considerations when working in the 'real world' outside of school.

Here the critical aspect is the focus on how engineering practice centred on solely technical solutions will be severely lacking for adequately addressing most situations involving people and how a more holistic approach is needed.

E: The need for engineers to be humble and open to critique

(The communication skills gained from the project) have allowed me to slowly begin to dismantle my own 'ivory tower of engineering' and to begin to fully engage with the issues I am examining on a much more holistic level... By stripping myself of the prestige of engineering I make myself vulnerable to critique as well. I consider this vulnerability to be central to a socially just design process. As flawless as the technical minutiae of a project might be, no design will ever be perfect in four dimensions. The design process must then incorporate a reflexivity that allows for it to change with time and conditions, be they social, physical or otherwise.

Here the critical aspect is the focus on how engineers need to realise that while they might identify as problem solvers they do not know everything and need to be humble and open for critique to be able to find appropriate 'solutions.'

F: The need to ask who do we, as engineers, engineer for?

When brainstorming ideas for a product design for our project I couldn't simply suggest for example a chair as I would normally do in a brainstorming session. I had to stop, think, and deconstruct my suggestion before suggesting it to the group. I had to think who the chair was for, was it useful for (people in country A)? Was there a market?, would (specific group of people out on the margin of society in country A) benefit from a chair? This differed completely from an engineering brainstorming session where I would suggest anything as long as it could be physically manufactured in an engineering context.

Here the critical aspect is the focus on how engineers really need to consider who they are creating solutions for, that is to say, 'Who is the audience?'

G: The world is confusing and how do we as engineers fit in?

I think the lasting impression is going be that I need to do a lot of thinking about what I'm going to do after I graduate. And I think as of most of these issues that aren't engineering issues, where you walk out and say okay one plus one equals two. You walk out of it feeling like you knew less than you did when you walked in and you have to do more research and you have to think about the issues more. So I do feel I'm going to walk out of it feeling, personally, that I need to think hard about what I'm going do after I graduate, but I also think I'm going, just in general, to feel like the world is more confusing than I thought it was.

Here the critical aspect is the question of how one as an engineer fits into a world which seems more complex and confusing than before and the growing realisation that most issues in the world are not engineering issues.

In summary, we can see some clear patterns emerging. As defined by the students' perceptions of what we were helping them to learn, engineering as seen through a lens of social justice requires engineers to:

1) be able to critique their own practice, so as to question assumptions behind the common sense of the dominant discourse,
2) to question who they are engineering for,
3) to move away from positivistic notions of one right answer to allow for pluralistic diverse ways of knowing and being,
4) to be humble, open to critique and question their role in society.

We did not define this beforehand. This was a real example of a liminal space in the flesh. We assisted students in their journeys, inviting them into the liminal space and this is how they described their heterotopia once they were there. The course is an interesting example of critical pedagogy. The students are clearly not the oppressed in society; far from it. However they are certainly able to critique their role in society, their role as students and the sorts of knowledge they are expected to learn in other classes. This is an example of the problem posing model whereby the learning is about developing a critical consciousness, not learning a prescribed curriculum. They were able to question (after Mezirow) 'habits of mind' using different 'frames of reference,' develop new 'points of view' and subjectively reframe their worldview. They were on a journey of transformation through the liminal space.

Chapter 3

Thought Collectives and Common Sense

Common sense within engineering

It can be argued, as within any community of practice, that engineering students as well as practitioners and educators live within some form of 'common sense' that they have developed from their teachers and books and from the external social constructs of their society. 'Maximise efficiency, reduce costs,' for example, is considered common sense by most engineers working in industry, and it becomes difficult to question assumptions surrounding this view. Students and engineers today largely work within and unquestioningly contribute to the policies and agendas of the socially accepted neoliberalist, pro-development standpoint. This equates technical development with human progress and assumes that all people in all countries around the world will benefit from implementing Western style industrialisation. If we are to enable students to develop a critical questioning ability, and to position themselves from a stance of social justice, questioning the efficacy of these developments, we need to understand how these common sense views of engineering are developed and attempt to deconstruct them. Only then are we in a position to help students question the real cost and benefits and for whom, of current developments and to consider alternatives.

We draw from Ludwik Fleck's work on thought collectives to help us frame our ideas. Fleck defines a thought collective as:

A community of persons mutually exchanging ideas or maintaining intellectual interaction, we will find by implication that it also provides the special 'carrier' for the historical development of any field of thought, as well as for the given stock of knowledge and level of culture. This we have designated 'thought style.'

People can belong to many different thought collectives, but according to Fleck:

The individual within the collective is never, or hardly ever, conscious of the prevailing thought style, which almost always exerts an absolute compulsive force upon his thinking and with which it is not possible to be at variance.

Fleck argues that stable thought collectives form around organised social groups (such as professional engineers), and that if a large group exists long enough, the 'thought style' becomes fixed and formal in structure. He also argues that the longer a thought has been conveyed within the same thought collective, the more certain it appears.

Related to this is the work of Michael Polanyi, who is best known for his ideas about tacit knowing. While Polanyi seems to have been more interested in the act of knowing rather than the nature of knowledge itself, others have used his ideas to focus on the latter by discussing tacit knowledge. One such example is Meyer and Land who identify tacit knowledge as one of the different forms of troublesome knowledge relevant for their threshold concepts framework, which was described in the previous chapter. In their work, they develop the idea that students find thresholds in their learning and tacit knowledge becomes a barrier and one potential cause of these, to the uninitiated novice. They link tacit knowledge to Etienne Wenger's ideas about communities of practice; for example different disciplinary communities have their own shared, unspoken understandings and ways of doing things.

Both Fleck and Polanyi hint at dominant ways of seeing or

understanding the world within a given community of practice or thought collective. This has obvious connections with the ideas of Gramscian 'hegemony,' or what seems common sense to a community.

Hegemony is considered a process of social control which is subtle in that it is not evident or even potentially conscious control, but it is carried out through the moral and intellectual leadership of a dominant sociocultural group. The most important element is that this hegemonic sense is regenerated by the community who accept it as common sense. Thus, the 'common sense' which a group of people share and understand is of course not at all 'common' to everyone.

We argue that engineering may be considered a particular community of practice, with an associated common sense and thought style. If engineers blindly accept, and do not question the 'common sense' that they work within, they will be part of a thought style that they were not even aware of. All too often engineers are not in a position to do this critical questioning, as they did not learn the skills in school or elsewhere.

To enter this alternative space there must be a willingness to encounter ideas from different sources, a safe space within which to experiment and try out different ideas, an awareness of different ways in which individuals learn and grow, plus the creation of new language and a different discourse.

A worked example from engineering

A classic encounter that can be described as entering a liminal space is when one is forced to examine taken-for-granted practices, 'common sense' and ideas and encouraged to think new and often challenging thoughts, whilst 'hanging out in the fog.' In the terminology of this book, the established thought style surrounding a particular issue is brought into question. The example described here fits this description and offers a number of other supportive insights into the nonlinear process of

37

learning presented throughout the text. It is both an important issue in its own right and an excellent example of the case we aim to present.

We refer to a recent book on the subject of the future of the car (*After the Car* by Kingsley Dennis and John Urry, researchers from Lancaster University in the UK) which has brought this to our attention in ways that we had not previously considered and utilises resources that one might not have thought relevant. The book presents the now familiar environmental arguments related to the theme: the problems of climate change and global warming; the threat posed by peak oil; population growth and particularly the rapid growth of megacities. Assuming one accepts the figures presented, it is clear that we are facing significant environmental problems to which the expansion of car ownership and use are major contributors.

The argument, however, takes the debate much further, and enters the territory of the role the car plays in wider economic and social life. Hence it states that there are five areas where we need to acknowledge that the car is so much more than a means of individual transportation. These are: the car as the exemplary manufactured object produced by the leading business sectors and iconic names in 20th century capitalism (for example, Toyota, General Motors, BMW etc.); in most households the car as the major item of consumption after housing; linkages with other institutions, industries and related occupations (for example, oil refining, road building, hotels, car sales and workshops, retailing complexes, design and planning); car culture as representing the 'good life' defined as being a mobile citizen; the car as being its own home environment in which the driver can move flexibly and riskily through dangerous and strange environments. Add to these the cost of the car both in terms of environment and human life (worldwide cars generate 1.2 million deaths and 20-50 million injuries a year, costing an estimated $581,000 million), and it becomes clear just how important the car is on many different levels. The car is a means of personal freedom to explore 'the open road'; a means of flexibility in terms of travel that cannot be replicated by public transport; that which determines where and how people live in relation to commuting times and distances and access to family; that around which cities are designed and developed, and thus possibly the dominant feature of 20th century western life until the advent of the Internet.

What the text, as a whole, then goes on to do is to present possible scenarios, which offer a critique of the present situation and shows how new and developing technologies could radically alter current practice. The book asks us to question our common sense about what a car is and can be. It has to be said that none of these are exactly optimistic, but one can see how they can be extrapolated from the evidence provided. The first the authors describe as local sustainability, where long distance travel becomes increasingly difficult and unusual and the focus is on local and low carbon forms of transport. The second scenario is regional warlordism where there is an implosion of mobility and different groups start to compete for the limited resources still available. One assumes that any notion of social justice through a fair distribution of access to the goods required, is likely to be severely damaged by this. The third scenario is 'digital networks of control,' a post-car system where there is a movement away from vehicles as being separate and autonomous to becoming parts of an automated and digital system centrally controlled and operated. There are obvious authoritarian implications of this scenario. The fact that there appears to be such a limited set of options is, according to the authors, the direct result of the system pathways determined by the car culture and economies of the 20th century and it may already be too late to avert the economic and environmental consequences of the culture that has served so many of us so well, but at a huge cost for the future.

So what is presented are the current thought style, established wisdom or paradigms surrounding the concept of the car as a means of individualised transportation, critiques on the basis of the likely consequences of a 'business as usual' approach, possible future scenarios, and thus a potentially threatening and uncomfortable liminal space where we are forced into unfamiliar territory. Thresholds or tipping points into other ways of behaving and thinking are also made explicit and which offer a challenge to what has become the norm in relation to the car culture.

What is of additional interest in terms of this book though, are the other intellectual resources upon which the authors draw, and which reflect the two other aspects of the process we have identified: those of constructing new models and of developing new language or discourse. Particularly significant are the central parts of the book which focus, in turn, on systems, technologies, organisations and models. One system drawn heavily upon is complexity theory: a relatively new and developing approach which emphasises the nonlinear nature of the way systems operate and has connections with the model of learning we are trying to argue for. The new language and unfamiliar ideas derived from this source are an excellent example of a how a new discourse can be developed which opens up other ways of thinking and acting. There are also links with some of the resources that we have found helpful in this text, notably the theories related to liminality and the work of Latour, Deleuze and Guattari, each of which helps us to make new connections between different aspects of scientific and social thought.

The later stages of the argument draw attention to the technologies and organisations and enter into the technical aspects of the issue and recent research in much greater detail. These create obvious links with the engineering aspect of our book, but also with the social, economic and political dimensions of the future of transport, which, again, relate to our concerns to argue for social justice as a threshold for engineering. It would be good to reflect more deeply upon the substance of this in order to enhance the argument that both this subject of the future of the car, and the approach adopted by this specific book, present excellent examples of the case we are aiming to present, but that must remain for another occasion. At this stage we simply offer this as an important working example of the need to challenge existing thought styles and accepted paradigms and then the ways in which the nonlinear process of human learning and social development we describe as a heterotopia creates the liminal spaces in which a critique can be launched.

A challenge to common sense

It has been argued that much of the way engineering is both presented and taught fits into an established intellectual framework, or thought style, which assumes the priority of capitalist objectives. So engineering in the service of people and in response to their needs becomes subsumed under the banner of the profit motive and interests such as short-term shareholder value. One could add to this that a similar framework now dominates in many other areas of human activity and that with the apparent victory of market values as the main criterion for success, it is becoming increasingly difficult to find areas of life that have not been infected by this virus. Oliver James describes this as the virus of 'Selfish Capitalism.'

In John's previous publications, arguments are presented building upon the work of James and others, to show how the encroachment of market values is now damaging whole sets of human relationships and understandings of social life. So, for instance, family life and the nurture and education of children, is being driven by the highly competitive atmosphere of contemporary culture. To stand up against the peer pressure of sending one's children to as many different activities as possible is to be seen as depriving them of opportunities to progress and to become successful. In higher education it is commercial values that determine research funding and the structures of departments. In health care likewise, it is financial criteria that shape what treatments are available to whom, alongside political concerns of winning the votes of specific chapters of the electorate. The impact of the global financial crisis and the decision by many governments to use this as the occasion to cut government spending, notably in the areas of welfare and public services, simply exacerbates these tendencies.

Hence one can see that there are many different types of what we might call an 'enclosure' and that the question of how to move beyond these is vital for human flourishing. The general argument of politicians that 'there is no alternative,' whether one is talking about deficit reduction and spending cuts, or setting priorities in education, needs to be challenged and shown for what it is, a convenient opportunity for policies being pursued for other reasons. There is an urgency then across the globe, for the enclosure created by human greed, for that is what it is at its basest, to be broken open in a heterotopia which offers genuine alternatives.

So how do we move beyond the dominant common sense? One way is to make explicit the thought processes by which we understand or interpret a particular situation. This clearly links back to earlier references to the subliminal predispositions, frames of reference and underlying assumptions that we each bring to any decision. Working from within a faith tradition, for instance, one is faced with the issue of the extent to which one relies on interpretations of what has gone before, and the authority which is attributed to those interpretations, in order to discern the right course of action in the current context. What is one doing when one refers back to a text in an attempt to justify a course of action taken many years or centuries later and in a totally different setting? The legal profession is faced with a similar question under the heading of precedence, and those who claim to be following a Marxist path may also appeal to the original texts and their interpretation to argue their case. Hence, the notion of hermeneutics raises very practical questions of how to use the sources of one's tradition to argue for or against a case for action. It is especially important to be transparent about this, as we do not wish to be simply replacing one thought style with another.

To offer the theoretical sources first, the main references we use here are the work of Heidegger and Gadamer. Two main arguments seem to emerge from the study of their work. First, there is no such thing as a value free or fully objective interpretation. So one can never definitively argue that 'the text says this' therefore this is the only or precise meaning of that text and from that one can make a judgement that X is the correct course of action. One cannot follow a linear progression from a text through to a contemporary decision. Second, and this is a related point: all interpretation starts from somewhere and on the basis of a position already held. This is not to say that this position or assumption will remain unchanged or unchallenged, but merely that the process has to begin from somewhere. So one addresses a text with a particular question in mind and/or with a set of beliefs or assumptions already in place. What we argue for is that this becomes explicit and admitted by the writer and the reader.

The result of this is that interpretation begins to look like a circular process rather than a linear one. Both Heidegger and Gadamer talk about a pre-understanding and set up the theory of the hermeneutical circle. One goes round this circle, or as part of a community of interpreters, we engage in this process, ending up back where we started but now seeing things differently. So other elements and experiences enter the process, including our own experience and engagement with context, and these then change the interpretations as the process proceeds. This is dynamic and constantly changing rather than a static 'once for all' exercise which offers definitive answers. Perhaps the main reason why a particular community of interpreters continue to refer back to their traditional sources of authority is to give them a sense of identity through this reference to common sources. So whilst many continue to search for definitive answers, we would argue, on the basis of the study of hermeneutics, that the reference to historic sources is more about establishing a common point of reference. Marxists might refer back to the writings of Karl Marx, Christians to the Bible and Muslims to the Koran, but to imagine that this, in itself, yields clear answers to all questions, is simply to misunderstand the nature of the process.

So there is no such thing as a value free interpretation, and all interpretation has to start from somewhere, even if this is not where it comes to rest; if it ever does come to rest. It is a continuing process, carried out in the context of one's own community, and, hopefully, in dialogue with other communities, and in the light of the current challenges and questions being faced. Engineers too face the question of how to deal with their tradition and to interpret its sources of authority, but in such a way that human flourishing remains or becomes the goal of that process. The important thing is to recognise the assumptions we are making and to be transparent about them.

The challenge in this process as described is to connect the contemporary with the historic and traditional in such a way that established sources of power could be questioned and inter-rupted if necessary. As we have already seen, considerable power rests with those who believe themselves to be 'in charge of' inter-pretation and therefore can tell others what they should believe and how they should act. So the issues of control, power, and what it is to be human, are once again to the fore in this discussion.

"I was involved with a significant practical issue which may ground this discussion. The area where I was working had been promised a new school building, the current one being of poor quality and not 'fit for purpose' dating back nearly 100 years. Somewhat reluctantly and with no previous experience of this role, I found myself being elected the Chair of the school's Parent Teacher Association (PTA), having ourselves young children at the school. At the same time, an edict came down from central government to county level that there had to be cut-backs and rationing in terms of local expenditure on education. Just at the point where contracts were about to be signed on the building of the new school, the County Council withdrew its funding and the project went back to the bottom of the list in terms of priorities. The anger and the impact of this in the immediate area can be imagined.

What were we to do? Should we just let this happen and accept the consequences for the school of having to wait another few years before the likelihood of any action, or were we to protest to see if the funding could be agreed by putting pressure on others? Having rapidly decided that the latter was the correct course of action, I suddenly found myself organising a public campaign, along with other members of the PTA committee, which involved issuing press statements, getting the local TV down to interview people, and generally raising the profile of the issue by stirring up as much trouble as possible! For two weeks I did virtually nothing else, but at the end of this intense period of protest we had made such a fuss that an arrangement was reached with the County Council that the funding would be found and the project would go ahead. Had we done the right thing and was there a cost involved in terms of the power struggles both local and beyond? Having fought other campaigns subsequently against the closure of rural schools with which I have been involved, I think I would do the same again. There is certainly always an issue of where more articulate, middle-class parents and groups are better able to fight their corner, mobilise the press and other contacts, and can get their voices heard above those whose needs might be greater. But when it comes to the allocation of scarce resources, which is what the welfare state is about, it is often the case that those who shout longest and loudest stand a better chance of being heard. So there are distinct ambiguities in the process of protest in this context. But what we also quickly discovered within the immediate locality, was that the 'young bloods' and 'hotheads' on the PTA had disturbed the local power structures and equilibrium of an establishment that was prepared to sit back and do nothing in response to this crisis. This was seen as an implicit challenge to that local establishment and the way we had gone about the campaign and then the fund-raising that followed, created significant tensions between the different age groups in the area. This was played out in an election for a parent governor where accusations of rigging the election were aimed at the PTA. This was a depressing and painful experience after the victory we had just won. It seemed that holding onto power was more important to some individuals than what was best for the community. The starting point for their interpretation of events, let alone their criteria for taking action, seemed a long way from the search for better facilities, which motivated the young families. There was no neutral interpretation, and the claim by the establishment to be offering that disguised a struggle to retain power. Once again, those who wished to retain control over others had been challenged by the liminal space others of us had created.

There was a personal cost to my work and therefore to my family of that campaigning in that the work we had done alienated other colleagues and exacerbated an already existing rift in the area between the establishment and the young families. Having previously chosen to 'sit on the fence' in that dispute, I found myself deciding to take sides and fight alongside my peer group. Becoming a divisive figure in that sort of faith context rapidly becomes unworkable, so, not long after this I moved to another part of the country where I was in sole charge and could put the previous experience to work with greater freedom." (John)

Chapter 4

Theories, Models and Metaphors of Change and Action

Thought models

In order to support our counter hegemonic journey out of common sense we have been using various thought 'models.' However, models always have their limitations as they are only ever an approximation of reality. In this chapter we look at various models which may help us with our journey into heterotopia, by presenting different ways of thinking, analogies or metaphors. Some of which will appeal to us more than others.

Chaotic models of learning

For example, despite being a useful tool, the threshold concepts framework and the idea of 'passing through a liminal space' has received critique regarding a perceived suggestion that the nature of learning is linear. Land (one of the originators of the theory) and colleagues, however, when discussing the potentially recursive nature of a learning process, speculate by drawing on the work of Deleuze and Guattari that maybe learning is, rather, 'rhizomatic.'

To (re)imagine our conceptual model of a liminal space (as seen in Figure 1) in more nonlinear terms we draw parallels to Deleuze and Guattari's discussion in the chapter 'Of the refrain' in *A Thousand Plateaus: Capitalism and Schizophrenia,* a text nonlinear in both its structure and nature. Deleuze and Guattari discuss three aspects of what they call the 'refrain': or chorus of our lives: those of 'chaos,' 'territory' and 'cosmos.'

If we now visualise our liminal journey as given in Figure 2, a preliminary state may be seen as a fragile area at the centre of our picture. This is the initial outline of a new conception of a phenomenon or way of seeing (1). While liminal space is a place of flux and uncertainty, the liminal state is a process of attempting to grasp the concept and create a semi-stable order in the 'chaos.' This is the creation of (temporary) 'territories' (2) outside of the fragile centre. The potential opening up to 'cosmos' (3) can be paralleled to seeing the world through multiple lenses, perhaps what we have been calling heterotopia.

Figure 2: The liminal flower: A nonlinear conceptual model for liminal space. Potential learner journeys generally start in the Chaos (1) at the centre and regularly continue on into different liminal Territories (2) to sometimes even continue on out toward the Cosmos (3).

A central idea is that chaos, and from it, order, can arise anywhere in the cosmos, that is to say all learners will not start their liminal journeys from the same position. Most learner journeys through the liminal space will begin in a state of chaos when learners fix their fragile centre points from which they will attempt to create ordered territories out of the chaos. These liminal territories can be imagined to stretch out from this chaotic core and to overlap with and merge into each other to varying degrees. Most of the time the territories will be temporary and learners will dismantle them again when moving to new territories. Deleuze and Guattari refer to this as deterritorialization. The exception from this is when a learner, for one reason or another, gets stuck, unable to move forward. Deleuze and Guattari observe that '(a) territory is always en route to an at least potential deterritorialization (for example, moving on toward new understandings), even though the new assemblage (content and expression) may operate a reterritorialization (something that 'has-the-value-of' home) (for example, getting stuck (maybe due to an illusion of feeling safe)).' At some point learners might break out from their last territory into the cosmos. If they then could look back at the 'space' they had travelled through, they would see a 'territorial flower' floating in the cosmic sea. At the centre is the chaos and out from it stretch overlapping liminal territories as the flower's petals. This 'liminal flower' is our re-imagined liminal space or heterotopia. The territories represent conceptions or fragments of conceptions. Movement out toward the flower's edge parallels movement to more complex conceptions and acceptance of diversity.

In this model, learning clearly is nonlinear in nature and the learners' journeys toward the cosmos will go in multiple directions and potentially involve much backtracking. In more complex learning situations, like the ones we frequently refer to in this book, it is probably better to think in terms of a journey out toward the cosmos that never really reaches a definitive end, but where perspectives continue to shift and understanding becomes more complex. This, we believe, is the heterotopia.

When crossing the threshold, it is as if a space has somehow opened up; the 'new' emerges in some way, even though we are then at a loss as to know how to explain or describe this. But it does seem certain that 'a space' does describe the condition, which makes this possible. It wasn't there before, or we were not aware of it before, and then suddenly it is. Are we talking about something that happens gradually, an emerging from the background as it were, or rather the radically new and unexpected breaking in from the outside? Was this whatever it is already there just waiting for a comprehensive formulation or expression, or is it 'something completely different' that bears no relation to whatever has gone before? We will see in due course that this is a contested issue within philosophy, one which has huge bearings on not just education but on political activity as well. The space can either be an internal one or can be one between people; inner or outer. This is our heterotopia. Michel Foucault coined this term to describe places and spaces, which function in non-hegemonic conditions and we are borrowing this term to describe our utopian goal: the space or place where socially just engineering, or any radical transformation, can take place.

The Poppy seed head model for change

We have also found a nonlinear metaphor to be useful for reflections on personal and community development. From within the more radical theological circles influenced by Freire and his work in South America this has developed using the notion of the hermeneutical circle. As discussed previously, specific locations on the circle are identified, described and then moved through as one supposedly approaches a further stage. So, for instance, one is supposed to move from the questions raised by direct engagement with an issue or project, into further analysis using resources from non-theological disciplines (sociology etc.), then into explicit theological reflection using the resources of scripture or tradition, and then back into the implications of this for direct action. Whilst one can recognise elements of this in real-life activity, such a model is inevitably schematic and misses much of the complexity of front-line practice. Things simply do not happen in such a neat and orderly fashion, and if one begins to teach this model to students as 'the way to do it,' there is a real risk that they will never be able to implement or understand what is involved.

Hence the model of a 'Poppy seed head' seems to be a better way of describing what happens in practice. A breath of wind or energy strikes a particular location or set of people and then seeds fly out in all directions, randomly and in a nonlinear fashion, and nobody can know let alone control what will happen as a result of this. Some seeds may take root and others will not, but that initial burst of energy had to occur before anything could change. So the process is nonlinear and no one person can be in control of it. But there is the need for some catalyst, be that a person or an event. This seems to be very similar to what we describe in our liminal space diagram above, and is also a more accurate description, than the hermeneutical circle, of what happens 'in real life.' Therefore we share an insight into the essentially random nature of this activity, but also the need for somebody to set these events in motion through direct and deliberate action.

Boundaries, lines of flight and nomad space

A further Deleuze and Guattari (D and G) concept that may be of use to us is that of the 'border' or the 'borderline.' Whereas boundaries are perceived to be hard edged or solid points of demarcation between different things or beings, D and G see borderlines as being fuzzy, diaphanous thresholds in which it is much more difficult to see clear cut differences and edges. Examples of this might be swarms, flocks or packs of animals where it is difficult to say where the edges are and the pack begins or ends. So there is movement, multiplicity, complexity and a constant shifting, which makes the overall phenomenon much harder to 'pin down.' One thinks perhaps of accounts of the difficulty of trying to get accurate counts of the number of people in megacities such as Hong Kong where so many people are on the move at any one time and the place never stands still long enough to really know for sure who is there in total. There is, however, always an 'outside,' a place beyond where the phenomenon or state of being does not hold sway or can be registered, hence it is not the case that everything simply merges into everything else, it is just that there is a greater fluidity and motion than our normal language often acknowledges.

Linked to the above and central to D and G's work is the idea of 'lines of flight,' and there are similarities with Ingold's notion of lines, strands, threads and meshwork. A line of flight is 'the threshold between assemblages, the path of deterritorialization, the experiment'; in complexity theory terms, a move that triggers a bifurcation or divergence. This is where getting hold of the ideas becomes more challenging, as D and G use other terms from what is almost their own private language to define each other. So one really needs to examine what they mean by 'assemblages, deterritorialization' etc. What they seem to be getting at is that there are points where existing combinations of things or beings, for instance, the swarm or pack as above, divide and begin to form into other combinations. This is what they call a bifurcation, a splitting and formation of a new entity. This is important as it suggests a movement beyond the threshold and into another state of being, although not necessarily in a human-creative context, although this would need to be seen like this also. This sounds to us similar to what John has been trying to describe as 'blurred encounters' in previous publications, where there is often a lack of clarity or clear definition, but change does occur as a result of the encounter. 'Conversions' from one religion or culture to another are quoted as absolute lines of flight and described as 'vectors of freedom,' or at least, freedom from. Once again, the general idea is that of movement and flexibility which is difficult to pin down or define.

A third major concept of D and G that is of great interest and links with the others is that of 'space,' not surprisingly perhaps, and the ways in which they talk about 'nomad space,' 'smooth space' and 'striated space.' In reverse order, striated space is that which is firmly bounded and controlled by some human power or authority, so perhaps it is the state which is attempting to determine what fits where and why, or maybe a scientific convention which tries to do the same in order to define and control. Smooth space, by contrast, is like the flat surface in which everything moves without inhibition or externally determined direction. Nomad spaces are more like places of resistance or dissidence where alternatives to the structures of striated space can be formed and survive. When Deleuze applies his nomad/State opposition it is possible to see that nomad space is smooth whereas state space is striated, or enclosed with walls, ordered. There are apparent political implications of this although this does not appear to be the main reason why Deleuze uses these terms as this does not refer exclusively to human life and social constructs. What D and G do not argue though is that one type of space is intrinsically preferable to another, this is just a different way of describing the world. So 'smooth space' will not save us, any more than 'nomad space' will or can. There is always both smooth and striated space. This feels similar to the idea of the string vest theory; both string and holes are required for this to function effectively. It is just that we would imagine that greater freedom and creativity would emerge from the holes and more fluid spaces than from the clear structures and defined processes. We also note from previous work on creative thinking that the creative process often needs a 'safety net.' This is a netlike structure, which rests below or around the actor, as with a trapeze artist, to allow more freedom in exploration of the self, without being paralysed by fear.

It is not possible to enter into the full depth and complexity of D and G's terminology in this book, but hopefully there is enough of a flavour of their work to show that their alternative conceptualisation of the world, both human and non-human, has insights and ideas to offer to the more specific concerns of education and creative thought. The sense of movement, of dynamic but complex interaction, and the limitations of attempting to 'stop the references circulating' in order to control and define (although it is acknowledged that this will happen and does have its place) is reasonably clear we would argue. Therefore this is a useful resource of stimulating concepts and ideas.

Evolution or revolution?

Philosophers have been deliberating for centuries on the process necessary to elicit radical change. This requires at least two different but related foundations. First, there needs to be a base line or agreed criteria by which to evaluate current practice and the vision of an alternative against which to measure what is happening now. There will be different visions from within differing ideologies, but often common ground between them as well. The ideal of human flourishing or of well-being is one such value. Deleuze talks about the difference between actions that are life-enhancing and those that are life-denying, and even though this then begs the questions as to which are which, we believe that this might provide common ground in the struggle for social justice.

The other foundation required is that of some notion of how political life proceeds and of what can realistically be expected of radical political activity and therefore of what form it ought to take. One of the key current debates refers to the works of Deleuze and Badiou. Although this might appear to take us into obscure and irrelevant philosophical territory, it is argued by Zizek that the differences between them are politically significant. Callinicos has previously also contrasted the two and suggested a similar tension.

Put simply, the issue is that of whether radical change is a matter of evolution or revolution. We then come to the concept of the 'disjunctive synthesis' to be found in the work of Deleuze: the bringing together of different or contradictory elements that cannot be forced or formed into some neat new pattern or supposed harmony. This is powerful because it feels like the experience of bringing into contact different groups or individuals who 'don't mix,' as well as the more intellectual side of such a process. In terms of the 'blurred encounters' image, there can be encounters in which there is no real connection or contact.

The philosophical background, can perhaps be summed up in the idea that this is a 'relation of non-relation,' an encounter as a result of which nothing apparently changes. One can argue however, that this is one possibility only and that it might be more helpful to say that there is no guarantee that anything will change, but that such an encounter can be open-ended and unpredictable. An interpretation of Deleuze by Badiou *Deleuze: the Clamour of Being*, offers a valuable insight into the disjunctive synthesis. Using the example of the Incarnation from within theology, Badiou says that in the encounter both sides change, but both also remain distinct. There is no new combined entity, which subsumes or swallows up each partner in the process, yet each is changed as a result of the encounter. This seems to be a crucial way of describing what happens when there is a real encounter. There may well be a blurring, but this is not the same as one appropriating or destroying the other. Both remain, but both are also changed. If one can indeed interpret the concept of a disjunctive synthesis in this way, then it has something to offer to our understanding of what happens in a liminal space.

Deleuze, therefore, would appear to be on the side of evolution as he sees the world as a series of interconnected and constantly shifting strands and lines of development, but with anything new emerging from what is already there rather than intervening from an 'outside' which cannot be identified within the present. His thought has been an influence on the works of Hardt and Negri and their post-Marxist interpretations of politics. If they are correct, then one ought to be able to identify some signs or prospects for change within current social and political movements. This is not easy given that traditional Marxist arguments about the proletariat are very difficult to translate into contemporary social formations. Where are the individuals or groups who stand at one remove, or possibly further, from current capitalist enclosures, and can be at the forefront of genuine political alternatives? Zizek has suggested that it is those on the margins of the growing megacities in the developing world, those now disenfranchised and dispossessed who are the vanguard of real change.

The authors of this book have some sympathy with this view and also some direct personal experience of working with such groups but whether there is enough coherence or power within these to bring about significant change is an open question. The alternative approach is that of Badiou, who is more inclined to see change in terms of what he calls an 'event,' that which cannot be predicted or determined in advance in terms of what already exists, but is only likely to be seen as such in retrospect. It is also less the result of a pre-planned and shaped movement of like-minded activists, although there is clearly a role for radical action within the overall process. His language is difficult to interpret and the examples he offers somewhat limited and extreme, but he does offer a counterpoint to Deleuze and Hardt and Negri that needs to be considered.

Deleuze certainly offers ideas and concepts consistent with our idea of a heterotopia, particularly through his use of unfamiliar discourse and terminology. His ideas take us out into unknown spaces and unfamiliar territory and therefore into the 'fog' or 'cloud of unknowing' that might be the location for new thinking and action, but his insights into how the radically new can sometimes break in from the outside are weaker than those of Badiou. On the other hand, if one is always waiting for those 'events' to happen without any idea of what they might be or even if one would recognise them when they happen, it does rather limit the opportunities and motivation for taking action.

So despite much commonality there is one key area of contro- versy, which is brought to the fore by disagreements between Deleuze and Badiou. Just to remind ourselves of the other key debates before we move into this though, those being the nature of the spaces within which creativity is more likely to flourish; the capacity of people to 'hang out in the fog' and to live with ambiguity and uncertainty; then the extent to which we are in conscious control of the creative process or whether much of this happen 'behind our backs'; and finally the need to search for or construct possible 'locations for encounter' or blurred encounters by introducing new and unexpected elements into a situation. Each of these begs another question which now needs to be considered: when creative stuff happens, is this because something completely new enters the scene or is the process more of a reconfiguration or new combination of already existing elements? Are we talking about evolution or revolution; conti- nuity or discontinuity?

The work of Deleuze and also that of Deleuze and Guattari together is clearly on the side of continuity and evolution as it focuses on ways in which what is there already moves into different shapes and states of being. It has been pointed out by Badiou that Deleuze in particular is influenced by the early 20th century philosopher Bergson as well as by Spinoza. Theirs is a way of thought that builds upon observations of the natural world and emphasises that change comes about through the encounters of what is already in existence. Badiou, by contrast, can be described as a formalist philosopher, drawing on ideas from mathematics and especially set theory in order to argue for a more detached and radical understanding of change.

We might of course question whether this is something of a false dichotomy and it is better to argue that one experiences examples both of continuity and of more violent and sudden creative activity, although it is important to recognise that it is not

so easy to combine the two as they rest on very different understandings of the nature of life and 'the way things really are.'
Philosophers refer to this as a discussion about ontology or the
nature of Being and then how this relates to individual beings.

So what does Badiou 'bring to the party' and does it move the
discussion forward? His work appears to have been influenced
by the events following the 1968 student riots in France, the great
hopes of a real political change that those heralded, and then the
subsequent disappointment and disillusion that set in once it
became clear that these hopes were not going to be realised.
What then happened is that many of the intellectuals who were
caught up in this and came from a Marxist camp, abandoned or
lost faith with their earlier beliefs and pursued other philosophical and political paths. For instance, what is often referred
to as 'Postmodernism' emerges out of the response to this
turmoil. Badiou, however, sees this as a betrayal and is
concerned both to analyse why others turned away from their
original convictions and to present arguments for retaining the
hope for radical change. It is important to understand this
background as it sets the tone for Badiou's work but also
highlights precisely the question that concerns us here.

Two main issues arise. Can one justify a concept of radical
change when much of the evidence within current political life
shows that it is immensely difficult, if not impossible, to
seriously alter the course of, to put a term to it, Western liberal
globalised democracy? Then there is a further question of what
human beings must be like and how they would have to be or
become if such changes were a realistic possibility. Both are
relevant to this discussion given the argument that a concern for
social justice is a potential threshold for the engineering world,
and the search for appropriate models of education and human
development.

Once again we must limit this to quick references and leave
the option of deeper investigation to the reader, but Badiou

comes up with the notion of faithful subjectivity, a fidelity to fidelity itself that somehow transcends the beliefs that people hold at any one time with a confidence that change is possible despite evidence to the contrary. He does not present the human subject as an autonomous individual always in control of circumstances and her own actions, but rather as a point of activity which can, sometimes unknowingly, contribute to 'evental situations' where change might occur. So there is some common ground here with the view that creativity is less of a conscious process, but rather something that occurs as and when humans become subjects by engaging in radical action. So faithful subjectivity is the actual presence of an alternative within a situation. It is these 'evental situations' which are Badiou's way of describing moments of radical change, but, it has to be acknowledged that he sometimes struggles to offer real life examples of this. How does one draw a distinction, for instance, between the French Revolution, the rise of the Nazi regime in Germany, the Russian Revolution and, of course, the Maoist revolutions in China?

So there are difficulties about Badiou's ideas, but he has still highlighted a real issue that Deleuze provides no answers to. If change only results from a recombining or reconfiguration of what already exists, how does one explain, let alone hope for or work towards genuinely new situations? Once we talk about liminal spaces or thresholds are we clear whether this is a matter of continuity or discontinuity, and, if it is the latter, where and how does the radically new emerge? Then we also have to decide how human beings contribute to or engage with the processes of change and development as that will affect how one designs or constructs educational programmes. The authors' inclination is still to argue that there is both continuity and discontinuity, a reworking of what is there already but with the possibility of the new and unexpected breaking in, but we recognise that the philosophical positions of Deleuze and Badiou make this difficult to hold.

Hence it is perhaps wise, not simply to dismiss Badiou's ideas on how things happen in the political world as there has been recent evidence that unexpected and unpredictable events do occur which can bring about radical change. The fall of the Berlin Wall and the overthrow of communist regimes in a number of countries in Eastern Europe would appear to be one example. It is interesting that Badiou does not refer to these, presumably because he sees them as retrograde steps that have led only to varying forms of capitalism. But they are surely examples of unforeseen developments that 'came out of the blue.' The events of February and March 2011 in Tunisia, Egypt and Libya seem to fit this description. Within the space of a few weeks and without any prior warning or suggestion that major upheavals were about to take place, successive governments have been toppled or challenged. Whatever the apparent explanations for this; high levels of unemployment, rising food prices for instance; nobody had predicted that this could occur. There has been talk as a result of a domino effect spreading through the Middle East and North Africa, of the fact that Arab nations are just as keen as others to see the back of oppressive regimes and the emergence of some form of democracy. A more recent example is the London riots of August 2011, which also appeared to arise with no warning. The impact of better communications and the rapid spread of news through the Internet, Twitter and other social media has also been mentioned, particularly in the latter case where Blackberry was at one point 'blamed' for the events, but it is perhaps too early to know how to interpret these events, let alone know how political life in these nations will develop over the months and years to come. It will only be a matter of time before the commentators begin to get to work on this and people like Zizek come up with their own specific interpretations of what has been going on and what it means. For the purposes of this book though, it is enough to say that there are occasions when politics resembles the picture painted by Badiou and one should not automatically rule out the possibility of revolutions, 'events' that come from nowhere.

What Zizek helpfully does is to take ideas from both Badiou and Deleuze. He suggests that the original revolutions such as the French and Russian still have a relevance today in that their moving ideas need to be resurrected, brought back to life in another form, their spirit kept faithful to in contemporary forms. This is not too far from Badiou perhaps, both in intention and form. But Zizek also suggests that to rely solely on these sources for radical thought and action is to limit ourselves unnecessarily and to underestimate the impact of less ambitious activity. It can also be the case that small scale, local, incremental action that appears only to be tinkering with the existing system, may turn out to be the location for more radical change, and therefore also offer signs of hope. The reality is that one cannot know in advance whether or not any particular movement or action, revolutionary or evolutionary, will yield genuine change for the better. Even apparently regressive political activity might become the spur or occasion for change, against the intentions and designs of its authors. The unintended consequences of actions and the uncertainty of the results of any human activity have to be taken into account once we enter this territory. One could suggest that sometimes to do nothing, to refrain from action, is itself a potential form of radical response, which might create the new and different. But it does seem more likely that attempts to take action, to enter the pedagogical process for instance, to try to develop new discourses and ways of thinking about the world, are more likely to create the context for change. It is in this spirit that the book is offered as a contribution to forging new possibilities for human social and political life.

A worked example from engineering

An engineering project in the UK which is the cause of major controversy serves as a platform for practical consideration of the above discussion. On February 28th 2011 the Secretary of State for Transport in the Coalition government announced proposals for a High Speed Rail network (HS2). On January 10th 2012 the Secretary of State for Transport officially gave the go ahead despite ongoing protests from groups such as STOP HS2. We will not attempt to track the whole story which is ongoing at the time of writing but the initial protests and debates are in focus here.

The initial stage of the project will be a new track from London to Birmingham with no stations en route, and that, it is claimed, will reduce the journey time by about 30 minutes. There are further stages planned, with two routes branching off to Manchester and Leeds, and, again, reduced travelling time to both these northern centres. The arguments presented in support of the project are very illuminating, particularly as they seem to keep changing as objections and challenges to the figures being presented are made public. One basic argument has been that so many other countries now have these high speed rail links that if the UK does not follow suit it will fall behind economically. Then there are the more detailed arguments about journey time, taking traffic off the roads and thus environmental benefits. Of late the ground has shifted again and the focus is on greater equality of economic development between the north and south of the country, which is a big issue given the impact nationally of the global financial crisis of 2008 onwards and the coalition's (Conservatives and Liberal Democrats) strategy for responding to this which involves massive cuts in public spending that may have a disproportionate affect upon northern areas.

This project has been talked about for some years and was first mentioned under the previous (Labour) government, so the question faced by its successor has been that of whether or not to continue this plan under straitened financial circumstances. It seems odd in some ways that it is continuing with this given its withdrawal of funds from other previously funded projects, but one can only assume that the supposed economic benefits are predicted to outweigh the costs and disadvantages. Without going into the details of the project we would like to highlight how it links to some of the concerns and ideas raised earlier in this book and this chapter.

First, we have talked about Gramsci's notion of hegemony and ways in which those in power try to impose interpretations upon others. A clear example of this comes through in the consultation process launched by the government for HS2. The actual questions are presented in such a way that it is very difficult to answer negatively and assume, without question, that the economic benefits of the scheme can be taken for granted. Other government reports on the project throw these calculations into doubt and make it clear that what is presented by way of figures is highly optimistic to say the least. Thus proposed passenger numbers would have to be much higher than currently experienced; costs are calculated at current levels for a project that will take two decades to complete; if all goes well; and the Cost Benefit Analysis as produced by some measures make it clear that no rail project of this scale can ever be financially justified. But no mention of this is made in the questions presented to the public and it is difficult to see how one can engage with the process in any truly critical way. This is an example then of an imposed interpretation being presented as a neutral and democratic process.

Second, although certain environmental benefits are flagged up, particularly those to be gained from getting people to use public transport, it is clear that the real arguments are to do with support for the economy and the bolstering of the current capitalist culture. One wonders quite who is going to be able to afford the prices on such a line, let alone want to travel non-stop to and from these particular destinations. Business people and politicians one might assume, but not ordinary passengers who want access to other stations in between. In fact there could be a detrimental impact upon services on other lines as their trains are reduced to force people to use the new line. Then one questions whether the reductions in journey times are now so significant even for business people as they can spend train trips usefully working on their laptops and other communications devices. There is a real fear that ordinary travellers are going to lose out as a result of this project. Figures for new employment, particularly in the northern towns, will probably form a key part of the government's argument, but it is hard to substantiate these which can only ever be optimistic projections. So this feels like the enclosure of the capitalist system at work and it is hard to see how the expertise of the engineering profession is going to induce greater freedom and social justice.

So how is opposition to this project beginning to develop and what sort of counter-arguments are being presented? Is any potential counter hegemonic move coming from the inside or from an external group and do we see territories forming as these groups move into new liminal spaces? A number of local groups have sprung up, particularly in the areas affected by the building of the new line. The actual route goes through swathes of fairly affluent countryside between London and Birmingham, including villages where people commute into either city and further afield and property prices reflect that proximity to the major conurbations. So one can argue that there is a fair degree of NIMBYISM ('not in my back yard') going on here as there will be harmful impacts upon people's property values, rural views, and the peace and quiet that people move out to the country to consume. There will also be an impact upon farmland and the value of farms in the immediate vicinity of the new line, plus some houses will inevitably be knocked down and communities brought under pressure. Even the fabric of ancient buildings, including churches, could feel the effects of the actual rapid and frequent trains travelling close by. Hence there is no shortage of opposition and no lack of counter-arguments available by which to oppose this project. Perhaps then an obvious example of

Foucault's theory of power and counter-power, arguing that everybody has the capacity and freedom to stand up against developments being imposed from above. 'STOP HS2,' which identifies itself as the 'National Campaign against HS2,' has a very short, sharp resistance slogan: 'STOP HS2: No Business Case, No Environmental Case, No Money to pay for it.' At the time of writing, it is still protesting, despite the January 10th decision.

What is most interesting perhaps is that this is opposition by process rather than by revolution and that the components being brought into this are already available, even if they are then combined and presented in unusual ways. So this is protest through democratic means since they are available, and by gathering together different groups with different interests and with differing political expertise.

It is also possible that the debates stirred up, often inadvertently, by matters of concern such as HS2, can become the catalyst for other movements and discussions and so must be taken seriously as potentially contributing to the heterotopia that we advocate in this book. In the 'real world' then, one encounters projects that illustrate the more theoretical material upon which we draw and which assist in analysing what happens in practice. HS2 will be a massive engineering and building project and raises the sort of questions that we wish to raise under the heading of social justice. For whose benefit is this project? Are the engineers simply serving the cause of capitalist development or is there concern for the people who will be adversely affected by these large-scale works?

Global and local scales of change

In John's recent work it has become ever more evident that even the apparently local appeared to be determined or influenced by the global, or, at least, decisions made or actions taken at a greater distance and remote from the immediate locality. The growing economic impact of China and India, for instance, was affecting businesses both small and large within the UK. It was becoming more difficult to interpret and analyse what was happening in people's lives without taking into account the impact of the global economy upon their work, their family lives and their capacity, or lack of it, to engage in voluntary activity. The blurring of boundaries now goes far beyond an immediate area. Environmental activists have been flagging this up for some time, with the awareness that policies and decisions in one country have an impact far and wide, and that the effects of climate change cannot be restricted to a specific area. An example of global impact would be the tsunami off the coast of Japan, in turn affecting the nuclear power plant and creating the risk of contamination of fish stocks, plus the problems of supply chains in the motor industry being hit by the loss of production in Japan itself and the subsequent loss of production in car factories in other countries. More broadly, senior and middle managers are frequently put under pressure to relocate to the developing economies thus disrupting family and community commitments, whilst jobs at a lower level are under threat because of the pressures of greater labour mobility and the apparent need to cut wages, and so on.

Put simply, these were our reasons for moving beyond the work of Derrida and Habermas and searching for a framework that was better able to offer some insights into a world where connections, interconnections and ever more blurred and complex encounters are becoming the norm. We became interested in the ideas of Deleuze and Guattari and, specifically, the notions of liminality and thresholds as they relate to the human capacity to learn, adapt and transform their thinking and practices. The language of enclosures and thresholds already encountered in the writings of Hardt and Negri who argue that there is no longer any outside to the global system, that we are all enclosed within the structures of a particular form of global capitalism and that thresholds can only be found from within.

As noted earlier, this becomes an important point of difference between the philosophies of Deleuze, Hardt and Negri, and then Badiou and Zizek, with the latter more inclined to see radical change coming about from outside rather than as an organic development from within. So, although one might continue in local involvements, the focus needs to shift to a concern for the interconnections and trans-local encounters that shape our lives, and to the continuing question which all the authors share as to the conditions which make learning, change and growth possible or more likely.

"A very particular set of questions and involvements was stimulated by the onset of the global financial crisis as it began in earnest in 2008, and as its national and local conse-quences are still being played out in the UK through government spending cuts in welfare and public services, higher rates of unemployment, particularly amongst the younger age groups, and a growing inequality between the very rich and the increasing numbers at the sharp end of this global crisis. I have been working with colleagues from the William Temple Foundation (www.wtf.org.uk) trying to analyse what is happening, to question the discipline of economics itself as it failed, in some cases, to grasp what was and is happening, and to promote policies and under-standings that would counter these growing inequalities (*Christianity and the new social order: a manifesto for a fairer future* by John Atherton, Christopher Baker and John Reader). One argument is that this is simply another of these recurrent crises in the capitalist system and a means of redistributing wealth and power once too many people gain access to the goods of global capitalism; effectively a form of rationing of that access and an exclusion of even the middle classes from former levels of affluence. If this is correct, there will be significant social, political and economic consequences in most countries that are not yet fully evident. This is bound to make its way down to the level of engineering along with any other professions and sources of employment and to increase the pressures to conform to a system that demands more for less and decreases the opportunities for creativity and real learning. On the other hand, it may also inadvertently stimulate greater resistance to the current global capitalist system, and thus lead to unexpected liminal spaces where innovation and imagination come into play." (John)

Why then Deleuze (and later Latour) in particular? Essentially because we need a way of understanding the world and the way that humans operate within it, as it is now, which acknowledges and describes the interconnections which are socially and politically dominant. The old language and discourse which emphasises individuality and presents social life as invariably disconnected and operating in isolation no longer seems adequate. Hence the attraction of some of Deleuze's concepts as referred to earlier in the book. His different understandings of space, for instance, as striated or smooth, his work which puts together different elements in assemblages and sees change as happening through different lines of flight, each suggest a more adequate conceptualisation of the interconnectedness and variety of encounters which are characteristic of a globalised world. One must guard against the lazy interpretation of Deleuze (and Guattari) as postmodern philosophers concerned only with flows as if they were some magic counter to the existing powers and structures of the system. Their work is more descriptive than normative and is now contributing to developments in disciplines as diverse as geography and the philosophy of science. It is our argument that some of their concepts can also contribute to this discussion about social justice and the conditions for learning.

Circulating references, matters of concern and values

Latour also contributes to the general processes that are of concern in this book. We have noted that much social injustice and marginalisation of groups occurs when one particular institution or power block attempts to impose a particular interpretation or set of values upon the rest. This is to do with control, order and structure, which, as even Deleuze acknowledges, one cannot do without and will always be a feature of human life. However, one way of guarding against the worst excesses of this process is the means by which we claim to establish the truth: what is to be trusted in at any one time. Latour suggests that we should understand truth as the process of circulating references. In other words, we need to keep the process open and in flux and the references circulating in order to prevent the closure and ossification of our beliefs and practices. This image seems to be another way of describing the creation of the liminal spaces that we are advocating. So rather than allowing the search for truth to become settled and static, we need to keep feeding in to any specific discussion further references, ideas, experiences. This may cause confusion and create additional complexity, but it is more likely to disturb the established and settled interpretations that we know can so quickly become a strategy for exercising power over others. Some of us have a nasty habit of doing exactly what Latour proposes and pushing conversations out into unknown territory, or bringing into them unfamiliar or unexpected ideas. We think this reflects the liminal flower process described earlier by the Poppy seed head. Keep the references circulating then!

A further area where Latour has something to offer is his argument that rather than talking about subjects and objects, we should change our discourse to think about 'things' in the sense of gatherings of different components and elements. In particular we need to reconfigure our understanding of relationships with the non-human, which is something that became very real for John through the experience of the Foot and Mouth outbreak and the relationships between farmers and their stock. The non-human are not in a straightforward way 'objects' to be manipulated or controlled, any more than other humans should be, but all life is part of moving and changing sets of relationships in which we as individuals play different parts according to circumstances. We are part of assemblages, gatherings that are themselves fluid and negotiable over time and space.

In the light of the above, Latour suggests that rather than concentrating on 'matters of fact' we should instead attend to 'matters of concern.' In other words, all the different components of any situation should be taken into account and we should resist the temptation to reduce our analyses and understandings to 'the facts of the case' or those things which appear to be objectively true. So, for instance, in our earlier discussions about the future of the car and the UK high speed rail link, we should acknowledge all the different levels of discussion and various factors that are part of the debate. Thus human feelings and responses, concerns about the impact upon the non-human, should have as much a part of this as the supposedly objective facts about projected passenger numbers and cost-benefit analysis. This is an expansion of the 'rational' and also an inclusion into the debate of all the beings affected by it; therefore itself an expansion of the Habermasian concept of democracy where all those affected should have a voice. This is also consistent with the vision of a just approach to engineering.

Latour suggests we must question the traditional fact-value distinction which argues that we need to establish 'the facts of the case' before any values are brought into the discussion. He says that this is to leave the introduction of values until too late in the process; the values need to be there from the very beginning. This throws into question all organisational attempts to control decisions by 'getting the facts straight' before issues of justice can be brought in. Facts and values are always already interconnected, and so claims to present a 'neutral' or objective case invariably disguise the capitalist or power-based values that are already present and exclude the introduction of alternative ideas. Once again, one can see much of this at work within engineering. Engineering is classically seen as value neutral and yet this is of course far from the case as seen in more detail in the worked example given below.

"To follow Latour's advice, then, for engineers to consider values at the same level as facts, would potentially cause a shift in the direction of the engineering project and its outcomes. As an example of this, a few years ago, I founded a not for profit organisation, 'Waste for Life' (wasteforlife.org). I used my engineering knowledge to support the autonomy of cooperatives of 'waste pickers' in marginalised communities in developing products from the waste they collected, thereby bringing a new funding stream to their activities. On moving to Argentina to set up the project, I was told by a development studies academic in Canada, to 'stick to the science.' This was a confusing message for me. Any engineering or applied science project, including recycling technologies, will always happen in a social context. You can choose to work for a large corporation who will make money for the CEO or shareholders, or you can choose to work with a group of individuals whose lives will change dramatically if their income increases threefold from 200 to 600 dollars per month. It seems to us that the choice is only in who you decide to work with and for. That what you ultimately create will be dependant on this and will not be, in some notion of objective reality, always the same, no matter where, who or when we choose to apply our knowledge (which itself will shift). The machine we ended up creating to do the recycling would never work in a Northern context as it would not produce enough widgets per hour in our consumerist competitive environment. However when you are faced with selling plastic at 80 cents per kilogram (36 cents per pound) or a product at 5 dollars with the same raw materials, there is no necessity to produce millions of products; just enough to make a decent income for the families within the cooperative. And the machine is affordable and relatively easy to manufacture. If I, as an engineer, choose to value people before profit, I can choose to lend my knowledge to a different group of people, and a different engineered outcome arises. I have entered heterotopia." (Caroline)

A worked example from engineering

Edgar Schein's model of organisational culture (*Artefacts* stand in relation to *Espoused Values*; *Espoused Values* stand in relation to *Basic underlying assumptions*) shows us how espoused values might relate to what we do and why we do it. The 'thought styles' and 'common sense' that we have been talking about underlie what we value and why. This will then influence what we do and how we do it as demonstrated by the artefacts of our lives.

Either personal or cultural, values are beliefs that influence our thoughts, feelings, actions and attitudes. Values evolve from human interactions with the external world. They are related to the norms of a culture, but they are more general and abstract than norms. Norms are rules for behaviour in specific situations while values identify what should be judged as good or bad. In any society and culture there are ways of thinking that we have called 'common sense,' which result from norms and turn into values.

We maintain that professions each have their own hegemonic values, which need to be exposed, articulated, owned and even transformed, if professionals are to act in a socially just manner. We are not talking about enculturation or indoctrination to a particular value system, but we are interested in freeing up the student or professional to realise what they value and why, and to make free choices about these values in the future. Michael Adams in his book *Fire and Ice: The United States, Canada and the Myth of converging values* conducted a huge study of social values in the North American continent. Adams developed question-naires to locate the prevalent social values of different groups of citizens in the USA and in Canada. From the data, he created maps, which showed potential differences between these groups, such as between US citizens and Canadians, between men and women etc. Inspired by this work, Caroline and others studied values of engineers and engineering academics and students in Canada and the USA. Questions and statements were created to capture various aspects of these values, which were subsequently used to form the basis of a questionnaire to which volunteer engineering professors and students were asked to respond. An example question is given here:

> Your company has decided to outsource your computer department to Southern India. Huge savings will be made on salaries as labour is much cheaper in Bangalore. Do you think this is a good idea?

It was hoped that the values of the respondent would emerge from the selected response to the question and the parameters they chose to explore. In some cases the responses were given verbally, as in an interview and in some cases the respondents wrote their answers down. It should be noted that as this study was to explore an emerging methodology, no attempt was made to compare professors' with students' responses, nor break down the data in any other way. We created a new values-map: The North American Engineering values-map (Figure 3).

CONFORMITY / AUTHORITY		
PROFESSION / ENGINEERING	Confidence in Big Business Confidence in Engineering Market Demand Family Motivation for Engineering Profession Power of Money Usefulness of the Work	Balance and Resolution Comfortable Mobility and Safety Ethical Governmental Regulation National Pride Survival Social and Moral Responsibility Safety and Training	**SOCIAL / SOCIETY**
	Dream of Engineering Career Enthusiasm for Technological Advance Financial and Material Success Fulfilment Through Work Honesty and Loyalty to Work Potential Impact of Engineering	Awareness of Ecological Health Belonging to the Global Village Critical View Empowerment of Individual Financial Security for Local People Humanity and Social Development Introspection and Empathy Intuition and Impulse Peace Social Learning Sustainable World	
IDEALS / AUTONOMY		

Figure 3: North American Engineering values map. Each of the four boxes represents a group of thematically related values.

In the map, the western axis is: 'Profession/Engineering' and the eastern axis is 'Social/Society.' On the left of the map, we place values that hold in focus and major importance, the Profession of Engineering. On the right side of the map, we place values, which hold in focus or major importance, social impact and society. The northern axis is 'Conformity/Authority' and the southern axis 'Ideals and 'Autonomy.' In the upper boxes we place values, which hold in focus authority, tradition, norms and expectations. In the lower boxes we place values, which are more focused on idealism and individual autonomous decision making, as opposed to 'swallowed' values of an external authority. In this way, those values in the top left or NW box relate to the authority of the engineering profession. Participants expressing these, value above all, money, career, profession, status, security and usefulness of the work they do or will do. Those values in the top right or NE box relate to the authority of society, the Government, nation state, religion, etc. Participants expressing these, value above all, national pride, law, government regulation and control. They are also ethical and believe in acts of charity towards less privileged members of the society; however they do these because of a sense of duty, rather than because of any ideals. Values in the bottom left or SW box relate to the profession of engineering but focus on ideals and autonomy within this. Participants expressing these, value above all engineering as their dream career, they are technological determinists who believe that engineering solutions will solve the world's problems. Values in the bottom right or SE box relate to societies, communities and social issues, as well as idealism and autonomy. Participants expressing these, have strong ideals and value people and the environment. Here we find those who focus on environmental sustainability and social justice as well as those who believe that we have a choice. It is possible once the methodology has been tested through future studies within engineering and beyond, that individuals or organisations could have their values mapped onto these frameworks and comparisons could be made between different groups and individuals. This would then be an important pedagogical tool, to help students consider whether they are in fact valuing what they thought they were, or whether they have unconsciously 'swallowed whole' values from parents, school, society, which they would freely prefer not to put at the forefront of their work. It is also possible that these maps could be used to help employees and employers think about their roles and impact within society and help organisations move towards more socially just actions. It is of course imperative that the maps are not used to 'type' people and create the very boundaries we hoped to break down. For the purposes of this book this initial study or methodology pilot clearly shows that engineering, indeed, is not value neutral!

Chapter 5

Engineering: Liminal Spaces and Heterotopia

Our own liminal spaces

After multiple words of multiple authors, we hope that the reader has some sense of why we bother to write about such apparently esoteric ideas, albeit that we expect everyone is in a different place within the liminal space of this book. Tools, whether a hammer, or models of ways of thinking, can help us do the job we want to do. But we have to know how to hold the hammer, position the nails, what we are building, where we want to build it and why. The same is true for our lives. Many of us are discontented with what we see around us. We blame economics, or politics or neoliberalism or our boss. But if we have no tools or the ability and insight to help us reconstruct a new community, we don't know what to do after our deconstruction. We are left with a pile of rubble. The tools we explore here are metaphors or models to support ways of thinking, which can be applied to any situation in flux. We demonstrate our journeys through the new ways of thinking in the hope that they may inspire you to take on similar transformatory journeys in other professional and community contexts. We aim to help you deconstruct *and* reconstruct in a continuous cycle of transformation.

What we wish to do in this chapter is to describe examples of our liminal spaces and journeys as well as a kind of heterotopia for engineering practice. It is not our intention to demonstrate what should be done, which would be a rather ironic mimicry of the methods being critiqued, but suggest that in describing our own stories, we might invite others to enter their own liminal space or join us in ours. Ultimately it will be many, many individuals who join together as a community, with multiple solutions and multiple pathways through the liminal space, and who will co-create what becomes the new world of any profession or community.

A journey to Heterotopia: Liminal spaces in moving towards an understanding of engineering and social justice

This will be the story of the (major) liminal spaces of Jens's life in relation to our overall story in this book. When we began the collaboration on this book we suggested that on some level our lives are constant journeys through liminality (or a series of liminal spaces). We think one can zoom in on certain liminal spaces, experiences or times in a life. In his research together with Caroline, Jens has explored liminality in relation to certain threshold (learning) experiences: engineers approaching social justice as a critical lens etc. In the story here Jens will focus on three main thresholds tied to his intellectual development that all involved liminal journeys that opened up new ways of understanding the world. The main point of telling this story here is to illustrate some potential challenges and rewards involved in a journey toward heterotopia.

Threshold 1: Into mathematics, science and rationality

"First, I have to go back to an early period of my life for which my recollection is a bit hazy. A memory from my early school days (around the ages 7-10) is an antagonistic relation to mathematics as I simply was not very good at it. There is nothing special about this. I know several people who have had similar experiences (although not too many of them ended up taking science related courses at university later in life). I think that I (at least after a few years in school) was diligent and tried my best, but most of the time doing mathematics was slow going. The clearest example of this was when we in the 4th grade started learning multiplication or at least were trained to improve our ability to do multiplication quickly through frequently reoccurring tests. We would have ten minutes to complete 50 calculations (from the range 1x1 to 10x10) and I would never complete the full set on time and likely had one of the lower scores in the class. In 5th grade the number of calculations was increased to 100 while the time limit remained the same. I guess that initially I didn't do much better, but during this year mathematics started to make more sense to me. Then in 6th grade the number of calculations remained at 100 but the time limit was cut down to five minutes. Despite this increased challenge I started to get high scores and overall started to do well in mathematics. It is likely that this change had much to do with my maturity, but clearly mathematics or aspects of it proved to be a threshold to cross for my younger self. The important aspect for this book is that this crossing opened up a new world to me when I was in 7th grade and I started taking physics and chemistry and in these sciences found a passion for learning and knowing. For the rest of my secondary school years this gave me a way to understand many aspects of the world and I developed a worldview anchored in rationality. If there ever had been any gods in my world they definitively died now. I imagine that the struggles involved in crossing this threshold helped to firmly cement this new way of seeing the world." (Jens)

Threshold 2: 'Deconstruction' of gender and sexual orientation (among other things)

"This is a more recent (and ongoing) liminal journey that has been important for helping me understand social justice in a broader sense than just in terms of distribution of wealth. To properly illustrate this threshold I think I need to provide some more of my personal background. I grew up in a small and mostly white community located in the southern part of Sweden (close to the demographic midpoint of the country). In addition to myself, my family consisted of my father, my mother and my younger sister. My father was, and is, progressive and insisted on sharing the responsibilities of housework and child raising with my mother. For example he stayed home with me for an extended period of time, which is becoming more common in Sweden, but was less common back then. In terms of division of labour in the home my parents shared many tasks, but also divided them up on the basis of knowledge and efficiency. To some extent this division of tasks followed a traditional male and female divide, but the thing I've taken away from it is that it is 'natural' for men and women to share housework. Awareness of gendered roles was not something that was discussed explicitly (at length) at home as far as I can recall. Thus, while I might have had a predisposition toward the socially constructed nature of gender from lived examples this still has been a bit of a threshold to cross, especially before I went to university.

A related, or maybe more correct, aspect of the same threshold was the range of possible sexual orientations (for example heterosexual, homosexual, bisexual and asexual) and not just their potential social construction. My parents raised me to be respectful to others, but sexual orientation was another topic we didn't speak of at any length and this was not a topic well covered in the sexual education provided by my school (I believe it is a bit better these days). In addition, it was first at university that I met openly gay, lesbian and bisexual people and my impression is that during the late 1990s and early 2000s most portrayals of 'alternative sexualities' in popular media were not much more than stereotypical clichés (maybe it is not much better today). Until then I accepted 'other' sexual identities and orientations than my own heterosexuality on an abstract, detached and general level. However, on a more local, personal and lived level it was challenging for me to become comfortable with and 'normalise' (to myself) 'other' sexualities than my own. Thus the threshold to cross.

Based on the description above I would not say that I was navigating a liminal space as much as being stuck at the threshold. It was not any university course or such that helped me to get 'unstuck,' but the people I have met, especially my friend Anna, who I first met during my engineering studies at Chalmers University of Technology in Gothenburg, and who constantly challenged my notions about gender and sex when we became friends. That we became friends and the impact this friendship had on my own development I partly attribute to having the right subliminal predisposition at the time. We would often have lively discussions on a range of topics over both beer and tea. Often when we should have been studying. I imagine that there was quite a bit of Latour's circulating of references going on. Anna, among many things, was back then and still when we last met, a strong feminist, an activist spirit and a non-conformist (for example choosing not to drink alcohol in a booze-heavy student culture). She did impress my younger self quite a bit and from our frequent conversations, which were quite Freirean in nature, I got a kind of parallel education to the technical one I was getting in the lecture halls, tutorials and labs. Sometimes I feel I learnt more outside than inside of classrooms." (Jens)

Threshold 3: Move into social science research, move away form rationality and exploration of the intersection of engineering and social justice

"Despite my growing interest in mathematics and science, whilst in upper secondary school I maintained an interest in social science subjects such as history, while the humanities and arts mostly remained threshold areas to me. I also developed, through interacting with friends and watching the news on TV, somewhat left leaning political views based around solidarity and some sort of distribution of wealth. These views were not very well articulated as I didn't read any books on politics, and was not active in political youth organisations or affiliated with groups such as Greenpeace. As I progressed through my engineering education my interest in the social side of science and technology increased while my interest in the actual subjects remained constant or waned. By majoring in the area of technical communication I found a path to complete my degree that also opened up possibilities for exploring the social aspects of science and technology. In my Masters thesis research I investigated engineering students' conceptions of technology by applying a qualitative research approach called phenomenography. This proved to be another nontrivial experience, as my scientific and technical training had not prepared me well for working qualitatively with interview data interpretation. I got stuck several times, but under the guidance of my advisor Tom I managed to continue to move into this new liminal space. However, this was just the start of a longer and (yet another) ongoing liminal journey. At the time my path forward was unclear, but I had gotten the idea that doing a non-technical PhD likely would be preferable to going and working in industry as an engineer (something I ended up doing for a short time anyway). Around the same time I got the advice from a colleague of Tom's, that doing a PhD can become a real struggle if one starts to lose motivation for one's project in a big way and therefore it is important to work on something one is passionate about. This is really good advice and worth bearing in mind if one is considering doing a PhD! An exciting opportunity to work with Caroline on engineering and social justice came up that I believed would ensure my ongoing motivation. This ended up to be both true and not true. My PhD project was very exciting to work on and I completed it within my given (well, just a bit extended) timeframe. At the same time I struggled quite a bit with motivation and self-doubt. According to Caroline of all her graduate students I am the one who has expressed the most self-doubt. While I at times felt a lack of belief in my own analytic abilities as a researcher, I believe that most of my struggles in this part of the liminal space were tied to the great freedom and autonomy I had and was expected to manage as a PhD student and less to methodological issues. Under Caroline's patient and encouraging mentorship and thanks to my own stubbornness the PhD became a great learning and growing experience and I crossed another threshold. Among threshold concepts scholars, ideas have been articulated that doing a PhD is in fact a liminal experience partly tied to the transition from a student to an independent researcher. This resonates well with my own experience as described above. However, I am sure that each journey through the liminal space of doctoral studies and research will be unique. For example, other aspects of my particular threshold involved letting go of rationality as my main way of understanding the world (some of the ways of thinking I developed when I crossed the first major learning threshold of my life, a bit ironic, isn't it?) and constant reflection and questioning of my own privileges, choices and way of being as I delved deeper into the various aspects of social justice and critical thinking. This latter aspect manifested itself when I found certain texts or readings a bit offensive (for example a few written from a radical feminist position) or guilt inducing (for example those touching on the conditions of the poor). This makes much sense as many of these texts were written to challenge the dominant discourse, highlight inequalities, generate discussion and often take the position of 'oppressed' minorities such as women, queer-gay-lesbian-trans-persons, people of colour, and I mainly belong to 'dominant' groups being for example male, white and able bodied. I think feelings of this kind are almost unavoidable when challenging one's own privileged position or becoming more aware of it. It is never easy! For me this process had already begun when I engaged with the second threshold described above, but it accelerated during the time I worked on my PhD. I think this experience also gives me some insight into the challenges (engineering) students face when opening up to social justice." (Jens)

That was part of Jens's liminal story. The road to heterotopia can, and often is, long and can involve multiple thresholds to cross, some complementary and mutually reinforcing (his second and third) and some contradictory (his first and third). Maybe conflicting thresholds like these can become sites of (some form of) Deleuze's disjunctive synthesis or the blurred encounters John writes about. Two contrasting perspectives might be brought together within an individual and in the process be transformed but not merged together. Experiences like this might provide a richer understanding of the world, but the danger is of course that the end result becomes a form of Orwellian doublethink. Regardless, it is always possible to start the journey and with effort reach heterotopia. We have met several people, especially in the last few years, who also navigate the interdisciplinary areas between the social sciences and engineering and the natural sciences in general and for some the intersection of engineering and social justice in particular, and who tell similar stories to the one Jens has told here. We have also seen students start this kind of liminal learning journeys in courses such as the ones Caroline has created and taught.

Describing a Heterotopia for engineering

The question remains as to whether, after deliberating upon the lens we might use to critique the profession, the theoretical notions of space and place that we might draw on to gather our courage to do something creative about how we educate future professionals, and thereby transform the profession, we have any better idea what we want to change the profession into. What does this socially just profession look like and are we not just being the same as any other dogmatic leader if we decide what this is in an undemocratic way? Wouldn't the best process be to ask the public what they would like? Yes but which part of the public and how do we get them to all agree? Engineering alone is clearly not going to solve all of the concerns and many defensive engineers and students react to this kind of discussion by saying 'its not our fault, its the economy, business, globalisation' etc. all of which may be true but none of which absolves our part in business, the economy and globalisation.

In our various musings over the years, together with the very active international network for Engineering, Social Justice and Peace (esjp.org), (which Caroline launched seven years ago and which has just hosted its seventh annual conference in Colombia) we have found Young's five faces of oppression a useful basis with which to describe the injustices we wish to avoid in our practice. So we are now going to adopt these faces as a way of exploring and describing a heterotopia for a new engineering practice.

A Heterotopia for engineering, Part 1: The deconstruction
Let us create an engineering heterotopia which:

1. Avoids any form of exploitation (benefiting at the expense

of others)

This includes exploitative labour practices (especially when traversing nation states where companies can trade outside their nation's labour laws), aboriginal titles and land use, where engineering companies will offer monetary reward to starving people for the desecration of sacred space, and pillage of natural resources, for example drinks companies using up local supplies of drinking water.

2. Avoids or reduces marginalisation (being pushed away from participation in social life)

This includes contribution to the division between haves and have-nots. This might be economic marginalisation, created by economic policies, enacted by and enforced by increased production and consumption, all of which are supported by engineering. It could also be technological marginalisation, whereby those who are unable to access the Internet become increasingly cut off from all forms of social life, education and knowledge itself, or developing equipment at very high prices to produce enormously high production rates, thereby cutting off small scale businesses and cooperatives. Innovation is often considered tantamount to 'high price.' Caroline was once told that developing a low cost machine for cooperatives, to achieve the same function as the expensive machine but at lower rates, would not be seen as 'innovative' by research councils. (This work continues to remain unfunded for these reasons).

3. Reduces powerlessness (being unable to make one's voice heard due to lack of status or respect)

This includes respect for different ways of knowing and knowledge, for example, farmers evidence on pesticides use, local communities' evidence on health effects of factories, Indigenous knowledge etc. but can also refer to the very notion of *who* we engineer *for*, whose needs are we serving? It is those in power who decide the policies under which engineering companies work, as well as what they engineer. This is usually that which will create the maximum profit, optimal lifestyle for the already powerful. Powerless voices might scream that the factory should not be placed here, or that they would like medicine for their child's tropical illness, or a very low cost machine to reprocess waste on a small scale, but if what they scream does not benefit the powerful, it rarely gets heard.

4. Eliminates cultural imperialism (the dominant culture becomes the way of interpreting social life)

   This includes the profession of engineering itself, where engineering-for-people, becomes engineering-for-profit: the dominant profit culture completely surrounds the engineer's view of what they must do for society. It also includes the rather more elusive concerns about our lifestyle and what has been coined 'technological determinism.' Our technologies are socially constructed (we create according to our current dominant social paradigms) but also technology then can determine how we live. Hence we create computers to help us do things faster but then we also find ourselves sitting in front of computers every day. The worked example in chapter 3 discusses one technology in detail: that of the car or automobile and its impact on our lives. This category also critically refers to the dominant culture on society for example white Australia dominating Aboriginal lifestyles.

5. Reduces violence (the risk and reality of being targeted with acts of violence)

   This final category is rather self evident. Engineering is completely tied up with the military. Most of our research funds come from military sources and we of course engineer all weapons and instruments of torture.

The above are the first, the most basic, non-negotiables for our heterotopia. To describe what we don't want; what we want to resist and escape from. To critique the established position and to describe the thought style. This is the deconstruction.

A Heterotopia for engineering, Part 2: The reconstruction

1. Community

    During the next stage of the journey we need to invite people to join us in our liminal space and consider theories, metaphors and models of change and action, as we have done in previous chapters. This is what we have done with the ESJP network; where each year we meet at the Annual International Conference to 'hang out in the fog,' to be in a safe space, to discuss things that are seen as politically incorrect in our usual domains. To allow ourselves the freedom of not knowing. Until such time as we might.

2. Action

    We need the support of this community to take action. To demonstrate to others what things look like when we do things differently. For this we need examples, we need to search out and find people who are already doing what we think needs to be done. Even if only partially, inexpertly, ineffectually (as yet), or on a very small scale. Engineers need to let the community know and to show them that they are there for them and not to exploit them. They need to engineer different things, for different people. And still survive economically.

3. Education

    Another element is to think about how we can educate students to be professionals for tomorrow. To question assumptions and common sense. To give them permission to not know all the answers or to solve all the problems, using their technical prowess. To realise that problems don't know disciplinary boundaries and that we all need help. That we cannot be the ones defining the problems for others, let alone the solution. We need educational materials that do not preach status quo.

"Together with anthropologist Rita Armstrong and filmmaker Eric Feinblatt, I'm presently conducting research of engineering practices as they encounter social groups. Borrowing from the traditions of ethnography, we are interested in mapping different responses to engineering projects. Mining in Indigenous Western Australia is our current study. We are interested in developing a visualisation of our own liminal space as we try to uncover the multiple truths of the mining executives, community negotiators and locally affected communities. We are attempting to move beyond the simple stereotypes of yes and no, such as the anti-mining movements who drive to protests in their cars made from iron ore and the companies intent in putting on the latest equivalent of 'green coating,' lets call it 'social make up' to please their shareholders. We aim to develop accounts of this heterotopia and invite engineering students into the liminal space of learning to help them become a more socially just, if its possible, (mining, civil...) engineer." (Caroline)

4. Critical reflection

Engineers or any professionals intent on transforming their practice towards one which closer approaches social justice, need to reflect upon the three following questions in relation to the hegemony of their workplaces and spaces:

a. Who are we working for and whose needs are we serving? Are we serving the needs of the powerless as well as the powerful? Are we respecting difference and diversity in the systems, service and products we create? Are we developing them in a participatory way? If not, why not and what can we do to change this?

b. How is the product, service or system created? Is it done in an equitable way? How can this be managed better and more equitably?

c. Who benefits socially and economically from any work done? Are we benefiting all in society? Are we eliminating any form of cultural imperialism by the products and systems we create? If not what can we do to change this?

5. Time

We need to allow ourselves space and time *to be*. Defining a heterotopia does not mean defining the solution or the goal. This will be co-created by all concerned. Heterotopia is described by a liminal space of uncertainty, whereby concerns are raised, questions are asked and time stops, trusting that the answers will emerge.

Chapter 6

Final Thoughts

In this short book we have done some very strange things. We have tried to describe a space which has no predefined terms, nor 'common sense' to hang our ideas on. A space, which the authors have entered, and over many years, have explored, alone and together. Through our conversations it became clear that what was critical for transformation of a professional discipline, was reflected in many different ways in highly theoretical tomes, as well as in very down to earth local community groups. We decided at one point that what we needed was a way to describe the necessary move from awareness of what was wrong, to belief in the change needed. It didn't matter whether you were believing in a God, or in social justice, or in an educational approach. At a certain point, you would know what the right thing to do was and you would do it. What we hadn't realised was that the very essence of not knowing, the space and place between awareness and belief, was what we needed to describe, to nurture and to appreciate. After years of 'hanging out in the fog,' waiting for the cloud to pass so we could reach our destination, we realised that we had already arrived.

Theory and practice go hand in hand. The more abstract ideas we have used in this book are of value to the extent that they inform our practice and shape our understanding of the immediate issues we face. We would also suggest that they are part of the ongoing debates about the way the world is and ways in which we, as humans, fit into that wider understanding. In particular, in order to counter instances of injustice and exploitation, we need to beware of interpretations, accounts and practices that claim to offer the final answers or the objective truth and instead to aim to keep the references and ideas circulating. We are not in control in the ways that we like to imagine, and it is rather in the liminal spaces where we may be confused and uncomfortable that the creative and unexpected begins to break through. Hanging out in the fog, entering our heterotopia, is actually the place to be, provided we can cope with that level of uncertainty. That, in itself, requires resources that we must work hard to develop and nourish.

Texts We Have Drawn Upon and Other Useful Reading

Atherton, John, Graham Elaine and Steedman, Ian, eds. *The Practices of Happiness: Political Economy, Religion and Wellbeing.* London, Routledge, 2011.

Atherton John, Baker Christopher, Reader John. *Christianity and the New Social Order: Manifesto for a Fairer Future.* London, SPCK, 2011.

Badiou, Alain. *Deleuze: The Clamor of Being.* Minnesota, University of Minnesota Press, 2000.

Badiou, Alain. *The Century.* Cambridge, UK, Polity Press, 2007.

Baillie, Caroline, Pawley, Alice L. and Riley, Donna. *Engineering and Social Justice: in the University and Beyond.* Purdue University Press, 2011.

Baillie, Caroline. 'Negotiating Scientific Knowledge' in *Entangled Histories and Negotiated Universals: Centres and Peripheries in a Changing world,* edited by Wolf Lepenies, pp. 32-57. Berlin, Campus, 2002.

Baillie, Caroline. *Engineers within a Local and Global Society.* San Rafael, California, Morgan & Claypool, 2006.

Baillie, Caroline and Catalano, George D. *Engineering and Society: working towards social justice.* San Rafael, California, Morgan & Claypool, 2010.

Baillie, Caroline, Feinblatt, Eric and Kabo, Jens. 'Whose project is it anyway? The case of Waste for Life, Argentina' in *Exploring Cultural Dynamics and Tensions Within Service-Learning,* edited by T. Stewart and N. Webster. Information Age Publishing, 2011.

Baker, Christopher R and Reader, John. *Entering the New Theological Space: Blurred Encounters of Faith, Politics and Community.* Aldershot, UK, Ashgate 2009.

Berger, Peter. *A Rumour of Angels.* London, UK, Penguin, 1967.

Bhaskar, Roy. *Meta-Reality: Creativity, Love and Freedom.* London, UK, Sage Publications, 2002.

Bonta, Mark and Protevi, John. *Deleuze and Geophilosophy: A Guide and Glossary.* Edinburgh, UK, Edinburgh University Press, 2004.

Callinicos, Alex. *The Resources of Critique.* Cambridge, UK, Polity Press, 2006.

Carr, Wilfred, and Kemmis, Stephen. *Becoming Critical: Education, Knowledge and Action Research.* London, RoutledgeFalmer, 1986.

Canadian Engineering Accreditation Board. Accreditation Criteria and Procedures. Canadian Council of Professional Engineers, 2008. Current version found at: http://www.engin eerscanada.ca/e/pu_ab.cfm.

Castells, Manuel. *The Rise of the Network Society.* Volume 1 of The Information Age: Economy, Society and Culture. Oxford, UK, Blackwell Publishers, 2000.

Catalano, George D. *Engineering Ethics: Peace, Justice and the Earth.* San Rafael, California, Morgan & Claypool, 2006.

Catalano, George D. *Engineering, Poverty, and the Earth.* San Rafael, California, Morgan & Claypool, 2007.

Engineering Accreditation Commission. Criteria for Accrediting Engineering Programs: Effective for Evaluations During the 2009–2010 Accreditation Cycle. ABET, Inc., 2008. Current version found at http://www.abet.org/eac-current-criteria/.

Claxton, Guy. *The Wayward Mind: An Intimate History of the Unconscious.* London, UK, Abacus Books, 2005.

Deleuze, Gilles and Guattari, Felix. *A Thousand Plateaus: Capitalism and Schizophrenia.* London, UK, Continuum, 2004.

Dennis, Kingsley and Urry, John. *After the Car.* Cambridge, UK, Polity Press, 2009.

Derrida, Jacques. *Writing and Difference.* London, UK, Routledge and Kegan Paul, 1997.

Derrida, Jacques. *Adieu: to Emmanual Levinas.* Stanford,

California, Stanford University Press, 1999.

Fleck, Ludwik. *Genesis and Development of a Scientific Fact.* Chicago, University of Chicago Press, 1979.

Foucault, Michael. Of Other spaces. 1967.

Foucault, Michel. *Discipline and Punish: The Birth of the Prison.* London, UK, Penguin, 1991.

Foucault, Michel. *The Order of Things: An Archaelogy of the Human Sciences.* Bristol, UK, Tavistock Publications, 1970.

Foucault, Michel. *The Archaelogy of Knowledge.* Bristol, UK, Tavistock Publications, 1972.

Freire, Paulo. *Pedagogy of the Oppressed.* London, Continuum, 2003.

Gadamer, Hans-Georg. *Truth and Method.* London, UK, Sheen and Ward Ltd, 1975.

Gewirtz, Sharon. 'Conceptualizing social justice in education: mapping the territory.' *Journal of Education Policy,* vol. 13, no. 4, pp. 469-484, 1998.

Gigerenzer, Gerd. *Gut Feelings: The Intelligence of the Unconscious.* London, UK, Allen Lane, 2007.

Habermas, Jurgen. *The Theory of Communicative Action,* Volume 1. Reason and the Rationalization of Society. London, UK, Heinemann Educational Books Ltd, 1984.

Habermas, Jurgen. *Moral Consciousness and Communicative Action.* Cambridge, UK, Polity Press, 1992.

Habermas, Jurgen. *Between Facts and Norms.* Cambridge, UK, Polity Press, 1997.

Hardt. Michael and Negri, Antonio. *Empire.* Harvard, USA, Harvard University Press, 2000.

Hardt, Michael and Negri, Antonio. *Multitude.* London, UK, Penguin Group, 2004.

Hardt Michael and Negri, Antonio. *Commonwealth.* Harvard, USA, Harvard University Press, 2009.

Harman, Graham. *Towards Speculative Realism.* Ropley, Hants, UK, Zero Books, 2009.

Heidegger, Martin. *Being and Time*. Oxford, UK, Blackwell Publishers, 1962.

Heidegger, Martin. *Identity and Difference*. New York, USA, Harper and Row, 1969.

Heidegger, Martin. *Poetry, Language and Thought*. New York, Harper and Row, 1971.

Gramsci, Antonio. *Selections from the prison notebooks of Antonio Gramsci*, edited by Quintin Hoare and Geoffrey Nowell Smith. New York, International Publishers, 1971.

hooks, bell. *Teaching Community: A Pedagogy of Hope*. New York, Routledge, 2003.

hooks, bell. *Teaching to Transgress: Education as the Practice of Freedom*. New York, Routledge, 1994.

Ingold, Tim. 'The Wedge and the Knot: Hammering and Stitching the Face of Nature' in *Nature, Space and the Sacred*, edited by Bergmann, Scott, Jansdotter and Bedford-Strohm. Aldershot, UK, Ashgate, 2009.

Ingold, Tim. *Being Alive: Essays on Movement, Knowledge and Description*. Routledge, 2011.

James, Oliver. *Affluenza*. London, UK, Random House, 2007.

Johnston, Stephen, J. P. Gostelow, W. Joseph King. *Engineering and society: challenges of professional practice*. Prentice Hall, 2000.

Kabo, Jens. *Seeing through the lens of social justice: A threshold for engineering*. PhD dissertation, Queen's University, 2010. Available from: http://hdl.handle.net/1974/5521

Kabo, Jens and Baillie, Caroline. 'Seeing through the lens of social justice: a threshold for engineering.' *European Journal of Engineering Education*, vol. 34, no. 4, pp. 315-323, 2009.

Kabo, Jens and Baillie, Caroline. 'Engineering and Social Justice: Negotiating the spectrum of liminality,' in *Threshold Concepts and Transformational Learning*, edited by R. Land, J. H. F. Meyer, and C. Baillie, pp. 303-315. Rotterdam, Sense Publishers, 2010.

Kabo, Jens, Day, Richard. J. F. and Baillie, Caroline. 'Engineering and Social Justice: How to help students cross the threshold,' *Practice and Evidence of the Scholarship of Teaching and Learning in Higher Education*, vol. 4, no. 2, pp. 126-146, 2009.

Kuhn, Thomas. *The Structure of Scientific Revolutions*. Chicago, USA, 1962.

Latour, Bruno. *Pandora's Hope: Essays on the Reality of Science Studies*. Harvard, USA, Harvard University Press, 2000.

Latour, Bruno. *The Politics of Nature: How to bring the sciences into democracy*. Harvard, USA, Harvard University Press, 2004.

Levinas, Emmanual. *Otherwise than Being*. Pittsburgh, USA, Duquesne University Press, 2002.

Meillassoux, Quentin. *After Finitude: An Essay on the Necessity of Contingency*. London, UK, Continuum. 2008.

McLaren, Peter. 'Critical Pedagogy: A Look at the Major Concepts,' in *The Critical Pedagogy Reader*, edited by Antonia Darder, Marta Baltodano, and Rodolfo D Torres, pp. 61-83. New York, Routledge, 2009.

Meyer, J. H. F., and Land, Ray. 'Threshold concepts and troublesome knowledge (2): Epistemological considerations and a conceptual framework for teaching and learning.' *Higher Education*, 49, pp. 373-388, 2005.

Meyer, J. H. F., and Ray Land. 'Threshold concepts and troublesome knowledge: Linkages to ways of thinking and practicing within the disciplines.' ETL Project Occasional Report 4 Enhancing Teaching-Learning Environments in Undergraduate Courses, 2003. Available from: www.etl.tla.ed.ac.uk/docs/ETLreport4.pdf.

Meyer, J. H. F., Land, Ray, and Baillie, Caroline. *Threshold Concepts and Transformational Learning*. Rotterdam, Sense Publishers, 2010.

Meyer, J. H. F., Land, Ray, and Davies, Peter. 'Threshold Concepts and Troublesome Knowledge (4): Issues of variation and variability,' in *Threshold Concepts within the Disciplines*, edited by Ray Land, J. H. F. Meyer, and Jan Smith, pp. 59-74. Rotterdam, Sense Publishers, 2008.

Mezirow, Jack. 'Learning to Think Like an Adult,' in *Learning as Transformation: Critical Perspectives on a Theory in Progress*, pp. 3-33. San Francisco, Jossey-Bass, 2000.

Pluth, Ed. *Badiou: a Philosophy of the New*. Cambridge, UK, Polity Press, 2010.

Polanyi, Michael. *The Tacit Dimension*. The Terry lectures. Garden City, NY, Doubleday, 1966.

Radin Dean. *Entangled Minds: Extrasensory Experiences in a Quantum Reality*. New York, USA, Pocket Books, Simon and Shuster, 2006.

Reader, John. *Local Theology: Church and Community in Dialogue*. London, UK, SPCK, 1994.

Reader, John. *Beyond all Reason: The Limits of Postmodern Theology*. Cardiff, UK, Aureus Publishing, 1997.

Reader, John. Blurred Encounters: A Reasoned Practice of Faith. Cardiff, UK, Aureus Publishing, 2005.

Reader, John. *Reconstructing Practical Theology: The Impact of Globalization*. Aldershot, UK, Ashgate, 2008.

Reader, John. *Globalization, Engineering, and Creativity*. San Rafael, California, Morgan & Claypool, 2006.

Riley, Donna. *Engineering and Social Justice*. San Rafael, California, Morgan & Claypool, 2008.

Rorty, Richard. *Philosophy and the Mirror of Nature*. Oxford, UK, Basil Blackwell Publishers, 1980.

Schein, E. H. *Organizational Culture and Leadership*. 2d ed. San Francisco, Jossey-Bass, 1992.

Underhill, Evelyn. *Mysticism: The Nature and Development of Spiritual Consciousness*. Oxford, UK, Oneworld Publications, 1993.

Voland, Gerard. *Engineering by design*. 2nd ed. Upper Saddle River, NJ, Pearson Education, 2004.

Wenger, Etienne. *Communities of Practice: Learning, Meaning, and*

Identity. Cambridge, UK, Cambridge University Press, 1998.

William Temple Foundation website: www.wtf.org.uk articles by various authors including John Reader and also the Religious Futures Network chapter of the site.

Wittgenstein, Ludwig. *Philosophical Investigations*. Oxford, UK, Basil Blackwell Publishers, 1972.

Yamun, N., Baillie, C., Catalano, G., Feinblatt, E., 'Engineering Values: An approach to explore values in education and practice.' In the proceedings of Research in Engineering Education Symposium, Cairns, Australia, July, 2009

Young, Iris Marion. 'Five Faces of Oppression,' in *Readings for Diversity and Social Justice*, edited by Maurianne Adams, Ximena Zuniga , Carmelita Rose Castaneda, Madeline L. Peters, Heather W. Hackman , and Warren J. Blumenfeld, pp. 35-49. New York, Routledge, 2000.

Zandvoort, H. 'Preparing engineers for social responsibility.' *European Journal of Engineering Education*, vol. 33, no. 2,133-140, 2008.

Zizek, Slavoj. *The Ticklish Subject: the absent centre of political ontology*. London, UK, Verso Press, 1999.

Zizek, Slavoj. *The Parallax View*. Cambridge, Massachusetts, MIT Press, 2006.

Zizek, Slavoj. *In Defence of Lost Causes*. London UK, Verso Press, 2009.

Zizek, Slavoj. *Living in the End Times*. London, UK, Verso Press, 2011.

Words Borrowed from Other Works and People

Throughout the text we have introduced ideas and terminology from other scholars and texts and utilised them on our road toward heterotopia. We encourage the reader to follow up on the names and titles we refer to and which can be found in the preceding section 'Texts We Have Drawn Upon and Other Useful Reading.' Occasionally we have borrowed the words of other people in the form of longer direct citations or quotations and here we give the full references for these. We list these references in order of appearance and group them by chapter and subchapter.

Chapter 1

Guy Claxton's definition of John Keats's 'negative capability' can be found at page 149 of his book *The Wayward Mind: An Intimate History of the Unconscious* (2005, Abacus Books, London, UK).

Chapter 2

What is this profession called 'engineering'?: Thomas Tredgold's definition of engineering can, for example, be found at page 26 of Johnston, Gostelow, and King's book *Engineering and society* (2000, Prentice Hall). The American Engineering Accreditation Commission's (ABET's) definition of engineering we got from page 2 of Gerard Voland's book *Engineering by design* (2004, 2nd ed., Pearson Education, Upper Saddle River, New Jersey). The Canadian Engineering Accreditation Board's view of engineering and engineering education can be found in their 'Accreditation Criteria and Procedures' of which the current version can be found at: http://www.engineerscanada.ca/e/pu_ab.cfm. Johnston and co-authors' definition of engineering can also be found at page 26 of their book *Engineering and society*.

Mapping out the critical lens: Donna Riley's 'definition' of social justice can be found at page 1 of her book *Engineering and Social Justice* (2008, Morgan & Claypool, San Rafael, California).

Critical theories of transformation within engineering education: bell hooks's explanation of the importance of critical thinking can be found at page 202 of her book *Teaching to transgress: Education as the Practice of Freedom* (1994, Routledge, New York). Her reflection on progressive education can be found at page 8 of her book *Teaching Community: A Pedagogy of Hope* (2003, Routledge, New York). Her thoughts about change and consciousness can be found at page 39 in the same book.

Transformations and thresholds: Jack Mezirow's definitions of frames of reference, habits of mind and points of view can be found at pages 16-18 of the chapter 'Learning to think like an adult' in his book *Learning as Transformation: Critical Perspectives on a Theory in Progress* (2000, Jossey-Bass, San Francisco).

Chapter 3

Common sense within engineering: Ludwik Fleck's definition of a thought collective can be found at page 39 of his book *Genesis and Development of a Scientific Fact* (1979, University of Chicago Press, Chicago). His thoughts about the impact of the prevailing thought style of thought collective can be found at page 41 of the same book.

Chapter 4

Chaotic models of learning: Deleuze and Guattari's discussion of deterritorialization and reterritorialization can be found at page 326 of their book *A Thousand Plateaus* (2004, Continuum, London, UK).

Boundaries, lines of flight and nomad space: The definition of 'lines of flight' comes from pages 106-107 in Mark Bonta and John Protevi's book *Deleuze and Geophilosophy: A Guide and Glossary* (2004, Edinburgh University Press, Edinburgh, UK).

Glossary of Threshold Concepts

These are terms found throughout the text which we have identified as 'threshold.' They are often troublesome to understand, have multiple meanings and can potentially transform us into new and different ways of thinking. Because there is no one simple way to define these we simply want to acknowledge their presence, signal their troublesomeness and invite the reader into heterotopia, to explore their meanings...

Appropriation
Assemblages
Blurred encounters
Circulating references
Common sense
Critical theory
Deconstruction
Deterritorialization
Development
Dialogical education
Disjunctive synthesis
Enclosures/thresholds
Encounter
(The) Enlightenment
Faithful subjectivity
Hanging out in the fog
Hegemony
Hermeneutics
Heterotopia
Human versus non-human
Liminal space
Liminality
Lines of flight

Matters of concern versus matters of fact
Negative capability
Neoliberalism
Plausibility structure
Poppy Seed Head
Positivist
Post-development
Postmodernism
Power versus counter-power
Rhizomatic
Smooth, striated and holey spaces
Social justice
State science and nomad science
Thought collective/style
Transformation
Wellbeing
Zones of entanglement

zero
books

Contemporary culture has eliminated both the concept of the public and the figure of the intellectual. Former public spaces – both physical and cultural – are now either derelict or colonized by advertising. A cretinous anti-intellectualism presides, cheerled by expensively educated hacks in the pay of multinational corporations who reassure their bored readers that there is no need to rouse themselves from their interpassive stupor. The informal censorship internalized and propagated by the cultural workers of late capitalism generates a banal conformity that the propaganda chiefs of Stalinism could only ever have dreamt of imposing. Zer0 Books knows that another kind of discourse – intellectual without being academic, popular without being populist – is not only possible: it is already flourishing, in the regions beyond the striplit malls of so-called mass media and the neurotically bureaucratic halls of the academy. Zer0 is committed to the idea of publishing as a making public of the intellectual. It is convinced that in the unthinking, blandly consensual culture in which we live, critical and engaged theoretical reflection is more important than ever before.